Free
from Lies

Also by Alice Miller

The Body Never Lies: The Lingering Effects of Hurtful Parenting

The Drama of the Gifted Child:
The Search for the True Self
(originally published as Prisoners of Childhood)

For Your Own Good:
Hidden Cruelty in Child-Rearing and the Roots of Violence

Thou Shalt Not Be Aware:
Society's Betrayal of the Child

Pictures of a Childhood:
Sixty-Six Watercolors and an Essay

The Untouched Key:
Tracing Childhood Trauma in Creativity
and Destructiveness

Banished Knowledge:
Facing Childhood Injuries

Breaking Down the Wall of Silence:
The Liberating Experience of Facing Painful Truth

Paths of Life:
Seven Scenarios

The Truth Will Set You Free:
Overcoming Emotional Blindness

ALICE MILLER

Free from Lies

Discovering Your True Needs

Translated by Andrew Jenkins

W. W. Norton & Company
New York London

For information about permission to reproduce selections from
this book, write to Permissions, W. W. Norton & Company, Inc.,
500 Fifth Avenue, New York, NY 10110

For information about special discounts for bulk purchases, please contact
W. W. Norton Special Sales at specialsales@wwnorton.com or 800-233-4830

Manufacturing by Courier Westford
Production manager: Anna Oler

Library of Congress Cataloging-in-Publication Data

Miller, Alice.
[Dein gerettetes Leben. English]
Free from lies : discovering your true needs / Alice Miller ;
translated by Andrew Jenkins.
p. cm.
Includes bibliographical references and index.
ISBN 978-0-393-06913-6 (hardcover)
1. Psychological child abuse. 2. Adult child abuse
victims—Psychology. 3. Psychotherapy. I. Title.
RC569.5.P75M56 2007
616.85'822390651—dc22

                                        2009007816

W. W. Norton & Company, Inc.
500 Fifth Avenue, New York, N.Y. 10110
www.wwnorton.com

W. W. Norton & Company Ltd.
Castle House, 75/76 Wells Street, London W1T 3QT

1 2 3 4 5 6 7 8 9 0

Contents

III

THERAPY: RESOLVING THE CONSEQUENCES
OF EARLY CRUELTY

IV

INTERVIEWS

V
FROM THE DIARY OF A MOTHER

Preface:
Telling Children the Truth

THERE IS STILL a widespread belief that children are incapable of feeling: either the things done to them will have no consequences at all, or those consequences will be different from what they would be in an adult. The simple reason advanced for this belief is that they are "still children." Only a short while ago it was permissible to operate on children without giving them an anesthetic. Above all, the custom of circumcising boys and girls and subjecting them to sadistic initiation rituals is still quite normal practice in many countries. Blows inflicted on adults count as grievous bodily harm or torture; those inflicted on children go by the name of upbringing. Is this not in itself sufficient and incontrovertible proof that most people have suffered serious brain damage, a "lesion" or a gaping void where we would expect to find empathy, particularly *for children*? Effectively, this observation is evidence in favor of the theory that all those beaten in childhood must have sustained subsequent damage to the brain, as almost all adults are more or less impervious to the violence done to children!

In my quest for an explanation of this fact, I decided in 2002 to find out at what age parents thought they might begin impressing the necessity of good behavior on their children by giving them "little" smacks and slaps. As there were no statistics available on this point, I instructed a survey institute to ask one hundred mothers from different strata of society how old their children were when they first decided it was necessary to make them behave better by administering slaps to their hands or bottoms. The responses were extremely enlightening. Eighty-nine of the women were almost unanimous in saying that their children were about eighteen months old when they first inflicted physical "correction" on them. Eleven mothers were unable to recall the exact age, but *not one of them* said that she had *never* struck her child.

These findings were published in the French journal *Psychologies* the same year. But they aroused no reactions of any kind, neither incredulity or indignation. My conclusion from this is that such treatment is widespread and its justification hardly ever challenged. The question it posed for me was what actually happens in the brain of a child exposed to smacking at such an early age. Though the pain inflicted may not be severe (at least we assume this to be the case), children will surely register the fact that they have been *attacked* by the very person they instinctively expect to protect them from attacks by others. This is bound to cause ineradicable confusion in the infant brain, which at this stage is not fully formed. Such children will inevitably wonder whether their mother is there to protect them from danger or is in fact a source of danger herself. Accordingly, they will adjust to the situation by registering violence as something normal and integrating it as such into their learning processes. What remains is fear (of the next blow), distrust, and denial of the pain inflicted on them.

What also remains is something I refer to in my book *The Truth Will Set You Free* as *mental blockades*. Later, in adulthood, the combination of infant confusion and the denial of suffering obviously instills reluctance or downright refusal to reflect on the problem posed by inflicting physical punishment on small children. Mental blockades (and the fear underlying them) prevent us from asking ourselves how this confusion originated in the first place. Accordingly, we fend off everything that would lead to such reflection.

As far as I know, what infants *feel* when they are physically attacked and the effects that the suppression of these feelings have on the life of individual adults and the whole fabric of society are issues that have never been addressed by philosophers, sociologists, or theologians. The lengths to which the evasion of these issues has gone struck me with full force recently when I was reading a superbly written and highly informative book on the subject of anger. The book describes with minute precision the disastrous effects of anger directed at scapegoats in the course of history. But nowhere in these four hundred pages is there any reference to the *origins* of such anger. At no point does the author indicate that the anger felt by *every individual person* stems from the primary, *justified anger* of the small child at the blows inflicted on it by the parents. The immediate expression of that anger is suppressed, but at a later stage this suppressed fury will be directed at innocent victims with uninhibited savagery.

As the torture of children and the suppression and denial of that torture are so widespread, one might assume that this protective mechanism is part of human nature, that it is designed to spare us pain and hence plays a salutary role. But there are at least two facts that militate against this interpretation:

> First, the fact that *suppressed abuse is passed on to the next generation* so that the progression of violence cannot be halted; and second, the fact that *remembrance of the abuse we have been subjected to causes the symptoms of illness to disappear.*

The established fact that the discovery of our own childhood sufferings in the company of an empathic witness (see pages 26–27 and 51) leads to relief from physical and mental symptoms (such as depression) forces us to look for an entirely new form of therapy. Unlike the denial of these sufferings—a recourse typically advocated by therapists—it is in fact the confrontation with our own painful truth that leads to liberation.

To my mind, this realization applies equally to therapy for children. Like most of us, I believed for a long time that children are in sore need of illusion and the denial of unpleasant facts in order to survive, simply because the painful truth would be too much for them to bear. But today I am convinced that, as in the case of adults, conscious knowledge of their own truth and the actual story of their lives will protect them from illness and disorders. But for that they require the help of their parents.

In our day and age there are very many behaviorally disturbed children and also very many therapeutic programs designed to help them. Unfortunately, most of these are based on the pedagogical conviction that it is both desirable and feasible to induce "difficult" children to become well adapted, obedient, and docile. What we are confronted with here is a more or less successful form of behavioral therapy designed to "repair" the disturbed child. Approaches of this kind willfully ignore the fact that problem children have invariably suffered a series of injuries to their integral personality dating back to the period between birth and the fourth year of life, the period in which the brain becomes fully formed. The history of those injuries is usually suppressed.

But we cannot genuinely help an injured person to heal their wounds by refusing to acknowledge them as such. Luckily, youthful organisms have better prospects of healing, and the same is true of mental lesions. Accordingly, the first step must be to look closely at those wounds, take them seriously, and refrain from denying their existence. The task in hand is not to "repair" a "disturbed" child but to minister to his or her wounds, something which can only be achieved by empathy and the conveyance of correct information.

Children need more than well-adjusted behavior for their emotional development and genuine maturity. They need *access to their own history* if they are not to fall victim to depression, eating disorders, or drug dependence at a later stage. It is my firm belief that, in the case of children with a history of physical abuse, even well-intentioned parental or therapeutic efforts are doomed to fail in the long term if the humiliations these children have been subjected to are never addressed, in other words *if they are left alone with their experiences*. To free them from this isolation—the feeling of being the sole guardian of a guilty secret—parents would need to summon up the courage to admit their errors to their children. This would change the whole situation. In calm and collected conversation with their children they might say something like this:

"When you were small, we hit you because we were brought up that way and believed that this was the right thing to do. Only now have we realized that we should never have done it, and we want to apologize. We are truly sorry that we humiliated you and inflicted pain on you. We shall never do this again. If we should ever be tempted to break this promise, we want you to remind us of this conversation. In twenty-three countries such behavior is a punishable offense; it is against the law. In the last few decades people have realized that beaten children live in constant apprehension. They grow up fearing the next blow. This interferes with many of their normal functions. Later they may be unable to defend themselves when they are attacked, or they may retaliate excessively in a state of shock caused by limitless fear. Anxious children find it hard to concentrate, both at home and at school. Their attention is directed less at the things they have to do than at the behavior of their teachers and parents, as they can never be sure when the next blow may be inflicted on them. Adult behavior appears totally unpredictable to them, so they constantly have to be on their guard. These children lose all trust in their parents, whose task it is to protect them from attacks by others and not to turn into aggressors themselves. Loss of trust in their parents makes children anxious and isolated because society takes sides with the parents and not with the children."

This information divulged by the parents is no revelation to the children because *their bodies already know all this.* But the parents' courage and their decision to look the facts in the face will certainly have a lasting beneficial and liberating effect. Also, this behavior will act as an important model for the children, demonstrating personal courage and respect for the truth and the dignity of their children, rather than violence and lack of self-control. As children learn from their parents' behavior and not from what they say, the effect of such a confession can only be beneficial. The secret the children have been left alone with has been given a name and explicitly integrated into the relationship, which from then on can be based on mutual respect instead of the authoritarian exercise of power. The unspoken injuries can heal if they are not left to fester in the unconscious. When children given this kind of information later become parents themselves, they will no longer compulsively repeat the sometimes brutal or perverted behavior of their parents, as the suppression of their injuries will not drive them to do so. The regret expressed by their parents has expunged the tragic events and deprived them of their malevolent after effects.

Children beaten by their parents learn from such behavior to regard violence as a viable expedient. This can hardly be denied. Nursery-school teachers would readily corroborate this view if they allowed themselves to see things as they are. Children beaten at home will take it out on their weaker classmates or siblings. In the family they are punished for such behavior, which leaves them completely at a loss. Isn't this what they have learned from their parents? In this way confusion sets in at an early age, later manifesting itself as a "disturbance." These children are then sent to a therapist. But no one dares to get down to the roots of the problem, although this would seem to be such an obvious course.

Play therapy under the guidance of an empathic therapist can help children express themselves and develop trust in the framework of a protected, consistent environment. But as such therapy hardly ever addresses the early injuries inflicted on the children, they are normally left alone with these experiences. Even the most gifted therapists cannot break down this isolation if, for the sake of the parents, they hesitate to include the injuries of the early years in their considerations. But their task is not to address these injuries themselves, as the frightened children would then expect punishment from their parents. Instead, therapists should work with the parents and explain to them why such exchanges could be liberating both for themselves and for their children.

Naturally, not all parents will respond to such a suggestion, even if it is recommended to them by a therapist. Many of them will scorn such an idea, accusing the therapist of naïveté, insisting that he or she has no idea of how devious children can be, and fearing that if they were foolish enough to fall in with this proposal their children would merely take advantage of them. Such reactions are anything but unexpected. Most parents see their own parents in their children. They are afraid of admitting an error because severe penalties were inflicted on them every time they made a mistake when they were children. They cling desperately to the mask of infallibility, and it is this that makes it so hard for them to respond.

But I am happy to concede that not all parents are such incorrigible know-it-alls. I believe that despite these fears there are many parents who would gladly desist from such power play, parents who would be prepared to help their children if their fear of a frank and open exchange had not prevented them from doing so. Such parents will presumably find it easier to address the "secret" that has been tormenting their children, and they will be rewarded for their efforts by witnessing the salutary effect that the revelation of the truth will have on their children. They will realize how futile the authoritarian preaching of values is in comparison with the honest confession of the errors they have made, a confession that gives adults the genuine authority that is born of credibility. Children require such authority because it helps them to find their bearings in the world. Children who are told the truth and are not brought up to tolerate lies and cruelty can develop as freely as a plant whose roots have not been attacked by pests (in our case, lies).

I have tested these ideas on my friends, and I have asked parents and children for their opinions. Frequently, I found that I had been misunderstood. My listeners assumed that I was talking about an *apology* on the part of the parents; the children replied that it must be possible to *forgive* their parents, etc. But this has very little to do with what I am getting at. If parents apologize, then their children may easily get the idea that forgiveness is expected of them, that it is their job to "let the parents off the hook" and free them of their feelings of guilt.

This is not the point at issue. What I have in mind is information that confirms the bodily knowledge of the children and focuses on their subjective experience. The children themselves are the essential factor, their feelings and legitimate needs. When children realize that *their parents are actively interested* in the *feelings* aroused by their physical attacks, they will experience a major sense of relief and also something like justice. The operative factor here is not forgiveness but the removal of secrets that have a divisive effect. The aim is to establish a new relationship based on mutual trust and to achieve the breakdown of the isolation from which these maltreated children have been suffering.

Acknowledgment by parents of the injuries they have inflicted on their children dismantles many barriers, and the effect is similar to a spontaneous healing process. This is something one normally expects of therapists, but they cannot achieve this without the help of parents. When parents display empathy for their children's feelings and own up to their mistakes without saying "your behavior drove us to it," then a great deal will change. The children then have something they can model themselves on. There is no attempt to evade realities, no attempt to "repair" them in line with the parents' ideas. They have been shown that truth can be put into words and, once expressed, has the power to heal. Above all, when parents admit their failings, their children no longer need to feel guilty for the mistakes their parents have made. Such feelings of guilt are the breeding ground for countless attacks of depression in later life.

Children who have sensed in such exchanges that their injuries and their feelings are taken seriously by their parents and that their dignity is respected are also more immune to the detrimental effects of television than those who harbor unconscious, suppressed desires for revenge on their parents and for that reason identify with scenes of violence on the screen. Politicians may envisage the prohibition of violence on television as a remedy, but this is unlikely to have much effect.

By contrast, children who have been informed about the early injuries inflicted on them will be much more critical of brutal movies or quickly lose interest in them altogether. They may even find it easier to see through the dissociated sadism of the moviemakers than do the many adults who are unwilling to face up to the sufferings of the maltreated children they once were. Such adults may be fascinated by scenes of violence without suspecting that they are being forced to consume the emotional trash peddled as "art" by filmmakers who are unaware that they are in fact parading their own histories.

This was forcibly brought home to me by an interview with a respected American film director fond of including repulsive monsters and sadistic sex scenes in his movies. He said that modern film technology had made it possible for him to demonstrate that love has many faces and that sadistic sex is one of them. He appeared completely oblivious of where, when, and from whom he was forced to adopt this confusing philosophy as a small child, and this ignorance is quite likely to accompany him to the end of his days. His self-styled "art" enables him both to tell his own story and to erase it from his memory at the same time. Naturally, such blindness has severe social consequences.

The best time for a conversation with one's children about the injuries inflicted on them is probably between the ages of four and twelve, at all events before the onset of puberty. In adolescence the interest in this topic will probably wane. At this stage defense mechanisms militating against the remembrance of early sufferings may already be firmly cemented, particularly as adolescent children will soon have children of their own and as parents can then experience a position of strength enabling them to completely forget how helpless they once were. But there are exceptions, and in adult life there are also times when, despite considerable success in their present-day careers, some physical illness may force people to face up to the questions posed by their childhood. Almost all the letters I find in my mailbox tell similar stories: "I was not abused, but frequently beaten and tormented. Despite this, I have managed to start a family of my own. I have children, a good job, etc. But now I have started suffering from depression, pain, and insomnia, and I don't know why. Could it have something to do with my childhood? But that was such a long time ago, and I can hardly remember anything about it."

It is by no means rare for people looking for answers to questions like this to discover their true selves, the story of a maltreated child and the pain he or she has been forced to deny. They start to live with their own genuine feelings instead of running away from them, and frequently they are astonished at the liberation they experience by pursuing this path. They give the child they once were what their parents were never able to give to them: permission to know their own truth, to live with it, to identify with it instead of fearing it. Because they know the truth about themselves they no longer need to lie to their bodies or to pacify them with drugs, medicines, alcohol, or ingenious theories. In this way they save the energy they once had to invest in fleeing from themselves.

THE LATER CHAPTERS of this book are made up of texts I have devoted over the last few years to the subject of inner liberation (through the reawakening of emotions such as fear, anger, and grief) and to issues connected with therapy. Some of them have already been published on my Web site. They are not chronological but are grouped according to the subjects they address, thus making it easier for readers to find their way around.

They consist of articles, interviews, and responses to readers' letters, ending with a narrative describing the liberation of a mother from the prison of her childhood and the constraints of social convention.

As the collection contains various articles designed as independent entities rather than parts of a book, the reader will come across a number of repetitions that I could not remove without jeopardizing the argumentation of the article in question. In the context of the present compilation, this means that some issues are addressed on a variety of different occasions. This was necessary to preserve the internal logic of the respective text.

I

~

THE
EXILED
SELF

1

Depression:
Compulsive Self-Deception

THE RUSSIAN WRITER Anton Chekhov has been one
of my favorite authors since my youth. I remember very
clearly the thrill with which I read his story "Ward No. 6"
at the age of about sixteen, enthralled by his acuity, his psychological sensitivity, and above all by his courage in squaring up to
the truth, calling it by its name and never sparing anyone he had
identified as a rogue.

Very much later I read his *Letters*, which, together with numerous biographies, provided detailed information on his childhood.
What struck me was the fact that Chekhov's admirable courage
in facing and telling the truth came up against its limits as soon
as his father was involved. Here is one of his biographers, Elsbeth
Wolffheim, on the subject of Chekhov's father:

> The disparagement and humiliation he was subjected to at school
> were as nothing compared to the repressions he suffered at home.

Chekhov's father was hot-tempered and uncouth, and he treated the members of his family with extreme severity. The children were beaten almost every day, they had to get up at 5 in the morning and help out in the shop before going to school and as soon as they got back, so that they had very little time for their homework. In the winter it was so cold in the basement shop that even the ink froze. The three brothers served the customers until late in the evening, together with young apprentices who were also beaten regularly by their employer and were sometimes so exhausted that they fell asleep on their feet. Chekhov's father . . . played a fanatically zealous role in the life of the church and conducted the choir in which his sons were also forced to sing.[1]

On one occasion Chekhov noted that in this choir he had felt like a convict in a penal servitude camp,[2] while in a letter to his brother he writes: "Despotism and lies have so thoroughly marred our childhood that it makes me sick and afraid to remember it."[3] Such remarks by Chekhov are extremely rare. All his life he was greatly concerned for his father's welfare, making major financial sacrifices to support him. No one in his immediate environment suspected that the suppression of the truth also demanded major psychological sacrifices of him. His attitude was generally considered to be that of a virtuous and dutiful son. But the denial of the authentic feelings caused by the extreme abuse he was exposed to as a child made huge demands on his strength and may have been responsible for the fact that Chekhov contracted tuberculosis at an early stage and also suffered from depression, referred to at the time as "melancholia." Finally he died at the age of forty-four.[4]

From Ivan Bunin's recently published book on Chekhov, *Tschechow*,[5] I learned that my ideas on this matter can in fact be substantiated by reference to Chekhov's own words. In the following quote he expresses high praise for his parents, although deep down he must have known that this was a massive distortion of the truth:

> For me, father and mother are the only people on this earth for whom I would do everything they asked of me. If I should make it to the top one day, this will be the work of their hands; they are splendid people, their boundless love of children puts them beyond all praise and outweighs all their faults.

Bunin tells us that on various occasions Chekhov said to friends, "I have never trespassed against the Fourth Commandment."

This betrayal of one's own knowledge is no exception. Repressed fear causes many people to entertain similarly erroneous judgments about their parents throughout their lives. In reality, this fear is the fear a very small child has of its parents. They pay for such self-betrayal with depression, suicide, or severe illnesses leading to an early death. In almost all cases of suicide, it is possible to establish that cruel childhood memories have either been denied completely or never identified in the first place. These people reject the knowledge of their infant sufferings and live in a society equally oblivious of this kind of distress. Even today there is still little or no room for knowledge about the fate of children and its significance for later life. This is why we are usually surprised when a celebrity commits suicide, thus revealing that he or she suffered from severe depression. The typical reaction from all sides is that the person involved had everything that other people wish for so dearly. So what can have gone wrong?

The discrepancy between denied reality and the "happy" façade struck me once again when I saw a documentary about the popular Egyptian-born singer Dalida, who suffered from severe depression for a long time and finally took her own life at the age of fifty-four. Many people were interviewed on the matter, and they professed to know her very well, to be very fond of her, and to have been very close to her, either personally or professionally. Without exception, they all insisted that Dalida's depression and her suicide were a complete mystery to them. Again and again, they said: "She had everything most people dream of: beauty, intelligence, incredible success. So why these recurrent bouts of depression?"

This complete ignorance on the part of all Dalida's closest friends and associates brought home to me the loneliness in which this star had spent her life, despite her many admirers. I assume that the story of her childhood would yield up an explanation for her suicide, but no mention was made of this aspect in the course of the documentary. Looking on the Internet, I found the information one nearly always finds in such cases: Dalida had a happy childhood and loving parents. The question of how she may have responded to the fact that she grew up in a convent school was studiously avoided.

From what I have read about such boarding schools, I know that it is by no means rare for children attending them to be exposed to sexual, physical, and mental abuse. They are instructed to understand this as a sign of love and care, which means they are enjoined to accept outright lies as something normal. I also know that attempts to publicize the scandalous conditions prevailing in such schools have been thwarted by the church institutions. Most of the former victims do everything they can to forget the torments inflicted on them in childhood, particularly as they know that in our society they will hardly find "enlightened witnesses"* prepared

---

*An "enlightened witness" can play a similar role in adult life to that of a "helping witness" in the early years. I use this term to refer to a person who is

to take their sufferings seriously. Only the indignation of others could help them to feel their own horror and rebel against these lies. But if assistance of this kind is so hard to come by, if all the authorities declare their solidarity with these lies, then depression is thrust upon the victims.

I have no way of knowing whether Dalida suffered such a fate. My remarks on this point are purely speculative and based on conjecture. But I have no doubt at all that the depression that assailed this successful celebrity indicates denied suffering in her childhood.

Many world-famous stars are in fact profoundly lonely people. As the example of Dalida indicates, they are misunderstood precisely because they cannot understand themselves. And they are not able to understand themselves because they grow up in an environment that displays no understanding for the sufferings of a child. Even in their early years they come in for a great deal of admiration. But admiration for a person's achievements has nothing to do with love and understanding. Hence the tragedy of childhood repeats itself, a tragedy never properly engaged with but fended off with the help of success and public acclaim. These people seek understanding by pinning their hopes to success; they take endless trouble to achieve it and to arouse the admiration of an ever larger audience. But this admiration cannot provide any real sustenance in the absence of understanding for their childhood distress. Because

---

aware of the consequences of neglect and cruelty in childhood. This enables the witness to provide support for individuals harmed in this way by displaying empathy for them and helping them to understand their confused and confusing feelings of anxiety and powerlessness as a product of their own early biographies. This makes it easier for them to identify the options available to them as adults (see also *Banished Knowledge*).

these stars deny this distress, they are unable to come to terms with it and spend all their lives starving for a mother's love and empathy. Despite the success they have made of their careers, life is meaningless because they remain strangers to themselves. And this self-alienation persists because they want to completely forget what happened to them in their early lives. As this is the way society functions, these stars are bound to remain misunderstood and are doomed to suffer the torments of chronic loneliness. Suicide appears to be the only way out of this misery. This vicious circle tells us a great deal about the mechanisms of depression.

The categorical denial of the pain we suffered at the beginning of our lives is harmful in the extreme. Suppose someone setting out on a long walk sprains an ankle right at the outset. That person may decide to ignore the pain and to soldier on because he or she has been looking forward to the outing, but sooner or later others will notice that their fellow hiker is limping and will ask what has happened. When they hear the whole story, they will understand why this person is limping and advise him or her to go and get their foot seen to.

But in connection with the sufferings of childhood, which play a similar role in our lives to a sprained ankle at the beginning of a long hike, things are very different. Those sufferings cannot be "spirited away"; they will leave their mark on the whole enterprise. The crucial difference in this case is that normally no one will take any notice. The whole of society is, as it were, in unison with the sufferer, who cannot say what has happened. It may well be that, despite the violation of their integrity, people who have been injured in this way really have no memories. If they have to spend their whole lives with people who play down the traumas of childhood, then they have no choice but to connive in this self-delusion. Their lives will progress in much the same way as the outing of the hiker who has sprained his ankle but pretends that nothing has happened. Should they, however, encounter people who know about the long-term effects of childhood traumas, then they will have the chance to abandon their denial and have good prospects of healing the wounds they have been carrying around with them.

Most people are not so fortunate. The celebrities among them are surrounded by hosts of unsuspecting admirers, none of whom recognize, or want to recognize, the distress afflicting the stars they idolize. This is in fact the last thing they wish to countenance. Some may have hoped for similar success in their own lives and cannot understand why celebrities cannot simply sit back and enjoy their stardom. Those who are particularly gifted may make use of those gifts to reinforce their defense against the truth and keep it hidden both from themselves and others. Examples are legion. We may recall the fate of the alluring Marilyn Monroe, who was put in a home by her mother, was raped at the age of nine, and was sexually harassed by her stepfather when she returned to her family. Right to the end she trusted to her own charm and nothing else, and finally she was killed by depression and drugs. Her own account of her childhood is frequently quoted on the Internet:

> I was not an orphan. An orphan has no parents. All the other children in the orphanage had lost their parents. I still had a mother. But she didn't want me. I was ashamed to explain this to the other children. . . .

Exceptions in this context are people who have suffered childhood traumas that were *not caused by their parents*. These people are more likely to encounter empathy in society because everyone can at least imagine what it must be like to grow up in a concentration camp or to spend horrifying days at the mercy of terrorists. To survive the consequences of experiences like these we need "enlightened witnesses" in society.

Such witnesses are usually conspicuous by their absence when the injuries in question were inflicted on the child by its parents. As adults, children abused by their parents remain isolated, not only from others, but also from themselves, because they have repressed the truth and there is no one to help them perceive the reality of their childhood. Society is always on the parents' side. Everyone knows that this is so, so children will hardly venture to seek out their own truth. Even if successful therapy helps them to experience and express their anger and resentment, they may well be confronted by the hostility of their families and friends. The readiness to attack them for violating this social taboo has to do with the fact that this violation is a source of major alarm for others too. They will sometimes mobilize all the forces at their command to discredit the former victim and thus keep their own repressions intact.

There are very few survivors of childhood abuse who are able to withstand such aggression and have the fortitude to accept the isolation involved in refusing to betray their own truth. As knowledge of the emotional dynamics involved in these processes increases, things may hopefully change, and the formation of more enlightened groups will mean that total isolation is not the only possible consequence.

But enlightened individuals are still rare, even among the experts. Anyone seeking information about Virginia Woolf on the Internet will be told by renowned psychiatrists that she was

"mentally ill," and that this had nothing to do with the sexual violence inflicted on her for years by her half-brothers when she was
young. Although Virginia Woolf's autobiographical writings give
a harrowing account of the horrors of her childhood, the connections between these severe traumas and her later depression are
still roundly denied today.

During her lifetime there was of course even less chance of
their being recognized. Although Virginia read these texts to a
circle of artistic friends, she was still doomed to her lonely fate
because neither she nor her environment, not even her husband
Leonard (as his memories of his wife reveal), possessed the key to
the significance of her early experiences. She was surrounded by
people who shared and encouraged her artistic ambitions, but she
was unable to understand the subjective experience of total isolation that kept on assailing her. Such an experience can ultimately
pave the way to suicide because the present sense of isolation constantly recalls the potentially lethal abandonment we experienced
as little children.

In 2004 the French publisher Fayard published a large-scale
biography of the Iowa-born film star Jean Seberg in novel form by
Alain Absire under the title *Jean S*. Jean Seberg starred in thirty-
five movies, some of them major successes (e.g., *Bonjour Tristesse*
and Godard's *Breathless*). As a child, she displayed a passion for
the theater and suffered greatly from the puritanical attitude of
her Lutheran father, whom she later idealized. When still at school
she was selected by Otto Preminger for her first film, *Joan of Arc*,
from thousands of candidates. Instead of sharing her elation at this
success, her father merely uttered dark warnings. He displayed
the same reaction whenever she was successful, preaching moral
sermons at her in the name of paternal love. All her life she was

unable to admit how much her father's attitude had wounded her, and she suffered horribly from the torments inflicted on her by partners she chose in accordance with a specific, recurring pattern.

Of course, we cannot say that her father's character was the cause of the unhappiness that marred her life. It was Jean's denial of what she suffered at her father's hands that sparked off her bouts of severe depression. This denial dominated her life and drove her to put herself in the power of men who neither understood nor respected her. The compulsive repetition of self-destructive partner choices derived from her inability to identify the feelings her father's attitude had aroused in her. As soon as she found a man who did not treat her destructively, she felt impelled to leave him. She longed for nothing more than recognition from her father for all the successes she had achieved. But all she got from him was criticism.

Obviously, Jean Seberg had absolutely no insight into the tragedy of her childhood; otherwise she would not have become slavishly addicted to alcohol and cigarettes and would not have had to commit suicide. She shared this fate with many stars who tried to run away from their true feelings by resorting to drugs or died early from an overdose, like Elvis Presley, Jimi Hendrix, or Janis Joplin.

The lives (and deaths) of all these icons indicate that depression is not a form of suffering that relates to the present, which after all has bestowed on them the fulfillment of all their dreams. Instead, it is the suffering caused by the separation from one's own self, abandoned early on, never mourned for, and accordingly doomed to despair and death. It is as if the body used depression as a form of protest against this self-betrayal, against the lies and the dissociation of genuine feelings, because authentic feelings are something it cannot live without. It needs the free flow of emotions in constant flux: rage, grief, joy. If these are blocked by depression, the body cannot function normally.

People resort to all kinds of "remedies" to compel the body to function normally all the same: drugs, alcohol, nicotine, pills, immersion in work. It is an attempt to avoid understanding the revolt of the body, to prevent ourselves from experiencing the fact that feelings will not kill us but, on the contrary, can free us from the prison we call depression. Depression may reassert itself once we revert to ignoring our feelings and needs, but in time we can learn to deal with it more effectively. Our feelings tell us what happened to us in childhood. We can learn to understand them, we no longer need to fear them as we did before, the anxiety recedes, and we are better equipped to face the next depressive phase. But we can only admit those feelings if we no longer have to fear our internalized parents.

The assumption I proceed from is this: For most people the idea that they were not loved by their parents is unbearable. The more evidence there is for this deprivation, the more strongly these people cling to the illusion of having been loved. They also cling to their feelings of guilt, which provide misleading confirmation that if their parents did not treat them lovingly then it was all their own fault, the fault of their mistakes and failings. Depression is the body's rebellion against this lie. Many people would prefer to die (either literally or symbolically by killing off their feelings), rather than experience the helplessness of the little child exploited by the parents for their own ambitions or used as a projection screen for their pent-up feelings of hatred.

The fact that depression is one of the most widespread disorders of the present day is well known to experts. The media also address the problem regularly, with discussions on the causes and the various kinds of treatment available. In most cases the sole concern appears to be finding the best psychoactive agents for individual patients. Today psychiatrists assert that at last medicines have been developed that are not addictive and have no side-effects. So the problem would appear to have been solved. But if the solution is so simple, why are there so many people complaining about recurrent depression? Naturally, some simply refuse to take pills on principle, but even among those who do there are many who are repeatedly afflicted by bouts of depression and are apparently unable to free themselves of this disorder, even after decades of psychoanalysis, other kinds of psychotherapeutic care, or recurrent hospitalization.

What does depression involve? In the first place hopelessness, loss of energy, extreme fatigue, anxiety, lack of impetus and interest. Access to one's own feelings is blocked. These symptoms may materialize in unison or in isolation, and they can afflict a person otherwise functioning normally, doing well at work, sometimes even taking an active interest in therapy and attempting to help others. But these people cannot help themselves. Why?

In my book *The Drama of the Gifted Child* (1979), I describe how some people manage to fend off depression with the aid of grandiose fantasies or extraordinary achievements. This applies very conspicuously to psychoanalysts and other therapists who in their training have learned to understand others but not themselves. In the book I trace this phenomenon back to the childhood histories of those who elect to go in for this line of work and indicate that they were forced at a very early stage to feel the distress of their mothers and fathers, to empathize with it, and to abandon their own feelings and needs in the process. Depression is the price adults pay for this early self-abandonment. These are people who have always asked themselves what others need from them, thus not only neglecting their own feelings and needs but never even making contact with them. But the body is aware of them and insists that the individual should be allowed to live out his or her authentic feelings and to claim the right to express them. This is anything but easy for people who in infancy were used exclusively to satisfy the needs of their parents.

In this way many lose contact in the course of their lives with the children they once were. In fact, this contact was never established in the first place, and access becomes increasingly difficult as time goes on. In the later stages the increasing helplessness of old age becomes a searing physical reminder of the situation they found themselves in as children. This is referred to as old-age depression and regarded as something inevitable that we simply have to live with.

But this is not true. There is no reason why people who are aware of their own stories should lapse into depression in old age. And if they do experience depressive phases, it suffices for them to admit their true feelings, and the depression will be resolved. At any age depression is nothing other than the escape from all those feelings that might bring the injuries of childhood back to mind. This leaves a vacuum inside us. If we have to avoid mental pain at all costs, then there is basically not much left to sustain our vitality. Though we may distinguish ourselves with unusual intellectual achievements, our inner life will still be that of an emotionally underdeveloped child. This is true whatever age we may be.

As we have seen, the depression reflecting this inner vacuum results from the avoidance of all the emotions bound up with the injuries inflicted on us in early life. The upshot is that a depressive person can hardly experience conscious feelings of any kind. The only exception is the case where external events may overwhelm us with feelings that remain completely incomprehensible because we have no knowledge of the true, unidealized story of our childhood years. We experience such a sudden outburst of feeling as an inexplicable catastrophe.

Patients turning to a psychotherapeutic hospital for help are repeatedly told that they must not think back to their childhood, that they will not find any answers there, that they should forget everything else and concentrate on coming to terms with their present situation. Highly significant is the care taken to ensure that these patients do not get upset and to prohibit visits from their relatives. Precisely because they act like an emotional charge for the patient, such encounters can have a revitalizing effect; the emotions thus triggered off are not harmful but in fact beneficial. But in the hospitals this view finds little response. Reading the correspondence between the poet Paul Celan and his wife, we sense the tragedy that such directives can cause in the lives of individuals. Celan was categorically denied visits from his wife in hospital, which only served to exacerbate his loneliness and the severity of his illness.

A spectacular way of shrieking out his loneliness to the world and telling the story of his childhood was devised by King Ludwig II of Bavaria. It is a well-known fact that this "mad" king ordered the construction of a number of opulent castles he never used. He spent a total of eleven days in one of them and never saw the others from the inside. These fantastic edifices were built with immense care and in accordance with the very latest principles of engineering. Today they are visited by countless tourists, admired by some, dismissed as kitsch by others, regarded by others again as bizarre excrescences spawned by a sick mind. During his lifetime Ludwig was labeled "schizophrenic," and this verdict has survived to the present day, although its explanatory power is in fact nil. What it suggests in effect is that absurd behavior is the consequence of a genetic defect and hence cannot be expected to make any sense.

Armed with this misguided knowledge, the tourists shuffle through the halls of these luxurious castles built by a "sick" king who misappropriated the taxpayers' money for his lunatic purposes. So far no one appears to have asked what happened at the outset of this royal life. Why did he build castles he never lived in? What was he trying to say? Was he trying to tell a story his body had registered only too well but his conscious mind had dissociated on the grounds that we must never accuse our own parents?

As firstborn son, Ludwig was subjected from the outset to a strict and rigid upbringing that made him into a lonely child starved of affection and human contact. This highly sensitive child was refused a spiritual home by his parents. He was considered stupid and left to the care of the servants. They at least gave him the food he was denied at the castle with the intention of making him learn to discipline his hunger. No child can understand the fact that such parenting methods are quite simply sadistic and reflect the course taken by the parents' own childhood. And even if the victim of such an upbringing should be able to understand these connections at a later stage, it would not do him much good: his body will insist that he actually feel his way through to his individual biography, to the genuine emotions that have been repressed. Throughout his life Ludwig II was unable to do that, hence his absurd behavior that was dismissed as "schizophrenia." The king was a "good son" who revered his parents, as is right and proper. He could never admit to his feelings of frustration and later directed his anger vicariously at his servants. The unacknowledged impotence of the child deprived of food in luxurious surroundings left him with one feeling only: anxiety.

This anxiety was the cause of his loneliness as an adult. He avoided other people, suffered from nightmares, feared that he might suddenly be attacked. It is more than likely that these fears can be traced back to real experiences in his childhood. Ludwig lived out his sexuality in secret. He was sent photos of handsome youths who believed they had been selected as models for drawing classes. But once these young men entered the king's chambers, they were sexually abused by him. Such abuse and deceit is unusual if the abuser himself was not abused in his youth. Accordingly, the conclusion that suggests itself is that Ludwig suffered sexual violence as a child. This need not necessarily have happened in the family. We know from the memoirs of the court physician Héroard what the French king Louis XIII was subjected to by courtiers in his childhood.[6]

None of this need have culminated in "schizophrenia" if there had been anyone in the vicinity of the adolescent king who could have helped him to recognize the cruelty of his parents' attitude and defend himself against it. But to achieve such insight he would have had to admit his anger and ask himself what it was that prompted him to have the castles built. Maybe he sought a creative way of referring to something he could never have allowed into his conscious awareness: the fact that as a child he was forced to live like a nobody, despite all the luxury surrounding him. He was ignored by his parents, his gifts were unappreciated (his father did not consider him interesting enough to be a suitable companion on his walks), and he was given so little to eat that he occasionally had to turn to peasants outside the castle in order to eat his fill. Perhaps the castles were designed to demonstrate to his father just how "interesting" his son really was?

Even when details about a person's childhood are well known, it is extremely rare for any connection to be drawn between these details and the adult's later sufferings. We speak of a tragic destiny, but we have little interest in understanding the nature of this tragedy. No one in Ludwig's entourage appears ever to have inquired into the deeper meaning of his castles. Though several films have been made about the "mad king," no inquiry has been made into the origins of his so-called schizophrenia in childhood. Numerous scholars have conscientiously sifted all the details available about his building mania and published books about it. The culmination of a person's delusions arouses keen interest, but the genesis of such disorders is passed over in profound silence. The reason is that we cannot understand such a process without pointing to the parents' cruelty and lack of affection. And this strikes fear into the hearts of most people because it threatens to remind them of their own fate.

This fear is the fear felt by neglected or tyrannized children at looking into the true, undisguised faces of their parents. It is the fear that incites us to self-deception and hence depression—not only isolated individuals, but almost all the members of a society that believes that medication has solved the problem once and for all. But how could this be possible? Most of the suicides I have mentioned took medication, but their bodies were not to be deceived. The body refuses to accept a life that hardly deserves the name. Most people keep the story of their childhood carefully buried away in their unconscious. Without suitable assistance, they will find it difficult indeed to establish contact with their early lives, should they wish to do so. They are dependent on experts to help them reveal the self-deception and free them from the chains of traditional morality. But if those experts merely prescribe medication, they are helping to cement that fear and also blocking off their patients' access to their own feelings, thus depriving them of the liberating potential implicit in this discovery.

Personally speaking, I owe my own awakening to spontaneous painting more than anything else. But this is not to suggest that painting can be recommended as a surefire remedy for depression. One painter I once greatly admired, Nicolas de Staël, painted 354 large-scale pictures in the last six months of his life. He went to Antibes to work on his paintings, devoting himself to them with searing intensity and forsaking his family for the purpose. Then "he plunged to his death from the terrace that had been his studio in those last six months."[7] At the time, he was only forty-one years old. The skill that so many painters envied him for did not save him from depression. Perhaps a few questions might have sufficed to set off a train of reflection in him. His father, a general in the years prior to the Russian Revolution, never acknowledged his gifts as a painter. It may well be that in his despair de Staël hoped that one day he might paint the decisive picture that would earn him his father's respect and love. Conceivably, there is a connection between his gargantuan efforts at the end of his life and this personal distress. Only de Staël himself could have found this out, if the decisive questions had not been taboo. Then he might have realized that his father's lack of esteem had nothing to do with his son's accomplishments but merely with his own inability to appreciate the qualities of a picture.

In my own case the decisive breakthrough came because I insisted on asking myself such questions. I let my pictures tell me my own submerged story. More precisely, it was my hand that did this, as it obviously knew the whole story and was only waiting until I was ready to feel with the little child I once was. Then I kept on seeing that little child, used by her parents but never seen, respected, or encouraged, a little child forced to hide her creativity so as not to be punished for living it out.

We do not need to analyze paintings from the outside. This would be of little help for the painter. But pictures can stir up feelings in their creators. If they are allowed to experience those feelings and take them seriously, then they can get closer to themselves and overcome the barriers of morality. They can face up to their past and their internalized parents and can engage with these things differently—on the basis of their growing awareness, not of their childhood fears.

If I allow myself to feel what pains or gladdens me, what annoys or enrages me, and why this is the case, if I know what I need and what I do not want at all costs, I will know myself well enough to love my life and find it interesting, regardless of age or social status. Then I will hardly feel the need to terminate my life, unless the process of aging and the increasing frailty of the body should set off such thoughts in me. But even then I will know that I have lived my own, true life.

2

Mommie Dearest

R ECENTLY, I SAT down to watch the film *Mommie Dearest* about the actress Joan Crawford, broadcast on the Franco-German television channel Arte. The film is based on the book by her daughter Christina Crawford, which I first read some twenty years ago. Initially, I had planned to write about the martyrdom that Christina went through in childhood and adolescence and the way in which the people in her immediate environment dispassionately observed her sufferings without lifting a finger to help or protect her. Her mother's husbands, the domestic servants, and her schoolteachers all had ample opportunity to see how the famous actress tormented, threatened, abused, tortured, humiliated, and exploited her daughter, but not once did they appeal to the mother to desist from this cruel treatment, accuse her openly, or undertake anything at all to save the child. This behavior on the part of society aroused my profound indignation, and I remember referring to the book in various interviews.

Now that I have seen the film for the first time, I also regard it as a graphic illustration of the subjects addressed in my previous book, *The Body Never Lies*, and my article "Morality and the Body." At the end of the film we see Christina standing at her mother's deathbed with tears in her eyes, saying, "I've always loved you, you've suffered so much, but now you are freed of those sufferings." This scene pinpoints the tragedy of abused children. Their own sufferings count for nothing. They have so completely internalized the determination of the parents and of society to ignore what they have been through that they can only feel compassion for their parents, never for the children they themselves once were. This is what we all call love.

What was this "love" but endless hope that her mother might change, endless waiting for some reliable show of affection, for reassuring tenderness, for the termination of fear and lies? Waiting for love is not love, even if we always call it that.

Christina is one of the few examples of people who are capable of representing their own truth, showing us her mother as she was and the way she treated her. Yet at the end she says "I've always loved you" because she misinterprets her desire for love as love itself. Luckily, she was able to free herself of this desire and lead a life that was meaningful both for herself and for others, precisely because she recognized her own truth. But very many abused children who confuse the desire for love with actual love run the risk of compensating for the absence of love with the help of their own children or their patients or other people dependent on them. This is why I find it so important for us to extricate ourselves from this confusion. Waiting for love is not love. It is an attachment that frequently makes it impossible for us to empathize with our own sufferings, thus leading to the kind of exploitation demonstrated by the actress Joan Crawford. She was cruel to her daughter because she lived in total unawareness. She could scream and weep and beg for compassion, but she could not understand that she was exploiting her own daughter because she was sparing her own parents, because she "loved" them in the same way as other abused children love their parents. This is an extremely destructive form of attachment, and the only way we have of escaping its clutches is by understanding the dynamic inherent in it.

II

From Victim to Destroyer

3

How Does Evil
Come into the World?

Today there can be no possible doubt that evil exists
and that there are people who are capable of extremely
destructive behavior.* But the fact that this is so is no
confirmation of the widespread assertion that there are people
who are born evil. On the contrary. The deciding factor is the
reception they are given when they come into the world and the
way they are treated later. Children who are shown love, respect,
understanding, kindness, and warmth will naturally develop different characteristics from those who experience neglect, contempt, violence, or abuse and never have anyone they can turn
to for kindness and affection. Such absence of trust and love is a
common denominator in the formative years of all the dictators I

*My definition of evil refers solely to the destructiveness of warped
individuals.

have studied. The result is that these children will tend to glorify the violence inflicted upon them and later take advantage of every opportunity to exercise such violence, possibly on a gigantic scale. Children learn by imitation. Their bodies do not learn what we try to instill in them by words but what they have experienced physically. Battered, injured children will learn to batter and injure others; sheltered, respected children will learn to respect and protect those weaker than themselves. Children have nothing else to go on but their own experiences.

Born Innocent

The well-known American pediatrician Dr. T. Berry Brazelton once filmed a group of mothers holding and feeding their babies, each in her own particular way. More than twenty years later he repeated the experiment with the women those babies had grown into, who now had babies themselves. Astoundingly, they all held their babies in exactly the same way as they had been held by their mothers, although of course they had no conscious memories from those early years. One of the things Brazelton proved with this experiment was that we are influenced in our behavior by our unconscious memories. And those memories can be life-affirming and affectionate, or traumatic and destructive.

In the 1970s the French gynecologist Frédéric Leboyer demonstrated that babies delivered without physical force and given a loving reception by their immediate environment show no signs of distress or any kind of destructiveness. In fact, they will even smile only a few minutes after birth. As long as they are not separated after birth, as was the custom in the 1950s, mother and child will develop a relationship of trust that will have positive repercussions on the further course of the children's lives. In the physical presence of her baby a mother will produce the so-called love hormone (oxytocin), enabling her to intuitively understand the signals emitted by the child and to care for her baby by a process of empathy.[1]

Why have these important, groundbreaking insights on human nature failed to penetrate into the awareness of the public at large? True, Leboyer's works have radically changed birthing practice all over the world. But the philosophical, sociological, psychological, and ultimately theological implications of his discovery of the innocent newborn child do not appear to have left any significant mark on society as a whole. The notion still persists that punishment—and notably the corporal punishment that goes by the name of "physical correction"—is both effective and harmless, although we now know that physical punishment actually creates the evil that we later try, more or less ineffectually, to banish by inflicting more of the same.

Evil Is Re-created with Every New Generation

In the Middle Ages there was a widespread belief in "changelings." The term referred to children of the devil smuggled into ordinary, well-meaning mothers' cradles in exchange for the babies they had actually given birth to. Though there is no indication of whom the devil is supposed to have sired these wicked, diabolical children with, or what he did with the good ones he spirited away, the fact is that the mothers of these changelings were instructed to bring them up with especial strictness, in other words to beat them black and blue, as this was the only hope of molding them into human beings worthy of the name.

Today we no longer believe in changelings, but most of us still believe in the efficacy of physical punishment, entertaining the idea that we can "beat some sense" into naughty children. Even Sigmund Freud was convinced that sadists take pleasure in torturing other people because they are insufficiently able to sublimate the death drive that he supposed to be innate to all of us.

Genetics provides an "updated" version of this belief in innate evil. It is frequently asserted that there are genes that drive some people to commit evil deeds even if they have had "lots of love" in their childhood. I have yet to come across such an individual. All the childhood biographies of dictators and serial killers that I have studied show them without exception to have been the victims of extreme cruelty, although they themselves steadfastly deny this. And they are not alone. Large sections of society are apparently determined to deny or ignore these facts.

Taken to its logical conclusion, genetic theory ought to be able to explain why, thirty years before the advent of the Third Reich, Germany should have brought forth millions of children whose genetic makeup was so badly contaminated that in adulthood they were willing to lend themselves to Hitler's atrocities without turning a hair. Why has there never been such an accumulation of rogue genes in Germany either before or since? It is a question I have asked repeatedly, and I have never received an answer. The reason is simple. There is no answer. Hitler's henchmen were victims of their upbringing. They belonged to a generation of children who had been exposed to brutal physical correction and humiliation and who later vented their pent-up feelings of anger and helpless rage on innocent victims. Safe in the knowledge that they were doing so with the Führer's blessing, they were finally able to give free rein to those feelings without fear of punishment. Today children are brought up very differently in Germany. But wherever cruelty and humiliation still play a part in parenting, those methods are faithfully reflected in the behavior of young people denying the pain of the humiliation they have been through, selecting and attacking scapegoats, and advancing harebrained ideological justifications for their depredations.

Genetic theory is just as incapable of explaining evil as is the changeling legend or the death drive. According to statistical surveys, a significant majority of the population of the world still believe that children need a "good" smacking from time to time if anything is to come of them. The truth is very different, and it is high time we faced up to it. Evil exists. But it is not something that some people are born with. It is produced by society, every day, every minute, incessantly, all over the world. It starts with the treatment meted out to newborn babies, and it carries on in the parenting methods practiced on small children. Such children may *become* criminal at a later stage, if they have no "helping witness"* to turn to. As I have said, there is no trace of such helping witnesses to be found in the childhood of dictators and serial killers.

---

*For me, a "helping witness" is someone who stands by a maltreated child (however rarely), providing support and representing a counterpoise to the cruelty that child experiences every day. It can be anyone from the child's environment: a teacher, a neighbor, a domestic employee, or the grandmother. Frequently, siblings play this role. The witness is a person displaying affection, or possibly love, for the neglected or abused child, eschewing manipulation in the guise of upbringing, trusting the child and giving him or her the feeling of not being "bad" and deserving kindness. Thanks to this witness, who may not even be aware of the decisive, salutary role he or she is playing, the child experiences the fact that there is something like love in this world. In the ideal case such children will develop trust in their fellow human beings and espouse affirmative values such as love and goodness. In the total absence of "helping witnesses," children will glorify violence and resort to it themselves in later life, more or less brutally and with the same hypocritical justifications they have heard from others. It is significant that there is no trace of "helping witnesses" in the biographies of dictators like Hitler, Mao, or Stalin.

4

What Is Hatred?

W E TEND TO associate the word "hatred" with the notion of a dangerous curse we need to free ourselves of as quickly as we can. An opinion also frequently voiced is that hatred poisons our very being and makes it all but impossible to heal the injuries stemming from our childhood.* I too believe that hatred can poison the organism, but only as long as it is unconscious and directed vicariously at substitute figures or scapegoats. When that happens, hatred cannot be resolved. Suppose, for example, that I hate a specific ethnic group but have never allowed myself to realize how my parents treated me when

* As my opinion on this subject differs greatly from the conventional view, I have frequently been misunderstood. Accordingly, my attempts to clarify the phenomenon of hatred and to give the term greater depth have not been very well received either. (See the chapter "What is Hatred?" in Alice Miller, *Paths of Life*, p. 150 ff.)

I was a child, how they left me crying for hours in my cot when I was a baby, how they never gave me so much as a loving glance. If that is the case, then I will suffer from a latent form of hatred that can pursue me throughout my whole life and cause all kinds of physical symptoms. But if I know what my parents did to me in their ignorance and have a conscious awareness of my indignation at their behavior, then I have no need to redirect my hatred at other persons. In the course of time, my hatred for my parents may weaken, or it may resolve itself temporarily, only to flare up again as a result of events in the present or new memories. But I know what this hatred is all about. Thanks to the feelings I have actively experienced, I now know myself well enough, *and I have no compulsion to kill or harm anyone because of my feelings of hatred.*

We frequently meet people who are grateful to their parents for the beatings they received when they were little, or who assert that they have long since forgotten the sexual molestation they suffered at their hands. They say that in prayer they have forgiven their parents for their "sins." But at the same time, they feel a compulsion to resort to physical violence in the upbringing of their children and/or to interfere with them sexually. All pedophiles openly display their "love" of children and have no idea that deep down they are avenging themselves for the things done to them as children. Though they are not consciously aware of this hatred, they are still subject to its dictates.

Such *latent, displaced* hatred is indeed dangerous and difficult to resolve because it is not directed at the person who has caused it but at substitute figures. Cemented in different kinds of perversion, it can sustain itself for life and represents a serious threat, not only to the environment of the person harboring it, but also to that person him/herself.

Conscious, reactive hatred is different. Like any other feeling, this can recede and fade away once we have lived it through. If our parents have treated us badly, possibly even sadistically, and we are able to face up to the fact, then of course we will experience feelings of hatred. As I have said, such feelings may weaken or fade away altogether in the course of time, though this never happens from one day to the next. The full extent of the mistreatment inflicted upon a child cannot be dealt with all at once. Coming to terms with it is an extended process in which aspects of the mistreatment are allowed into our consciousness one after the other, thus rekindling the feeling of hatred. But in such cases hatred is not dangerous. It is a logical consequence of what happened to us, a consequence only fully perceived by the adult, whereas the child was forced to tolerate it in silence for years.

Alongside reactive hatred of the parents and latent hatred deflected onto scapegoats, there is also the *justified* hatred for a person tormenting us in the present, either physically or mentally, a person we are at the mercy of and either cannot free ourselves of, or at least believe that we cannot. As long as we are in such a state of dependency, or think we are, then hatred is the inevitable outcome. It is hardly conceivable that a person being tortured will not feel hatred for the torturer. If we deny ourselves this feeling, we will suffer from physical symptoms. The biographies of Christian martyrs are full of descriptions of the dreadful ailments they suffered from, and a significant portion of them are skin diseases. This is how the body defends itself against self-betrayal. These "saints" were enjoined to forgive their tormentors, to "turn the other cheek," but their inflamed skin was a clear indication of the extreme anger and resentment they were suppressing.

Once such victims have managed to free themselves from the

power of their tormentors, they will not have to live with this hatred day in, day out. Of course, the memories of their impotence and the horrors they went through may well up again on occasion. But it is probable that the intensity of their hatred will be tempered as time goes on. (I have discussed this aspect in more detail in *The Body Never Lies*.)

Hatred is a very strong and assertive feeling, a sign of our vitality. So if we try to suppress it, there will be a price to pay. Hatred tries to tell us something about the injuries we have been subjected to, and also about ourselves, our values, our specific sensitivity. We must learn to pay heed to it and understand the message it conveys. If we can do that, we no longer need to fear hatred. If we hate hypocrisy, insincerity, and mendacity, then we grant ourselves the right to fight them wherever we can, or to withdraw from people who only trust in lies. But if we pretend that we are impervious to these things, then we are betraying ourselves.

The almost universal, but in fact highly destructive, injunction to forgive our "trespassers" encourages such self-betrayal. Religion and traditional morality constantly prize forgiveness as a virtue, and in numerous forms of therapy it is erroneously recommended as a path to "healing." But it is easy to demonstrate that neither prayer nor autosuggestive exercises in "positive thinking" are able to counteract the body's justified and vital responses to humiliations and other injuries to our integrity inflicted on us in early childhood. The martyrs' crippling ailments are a clear indication of the price they had to pay for the denial of their feelings. So would it not be simpler to ask whom this hatred is directed at, and to recognize why it is in fact justified? Then we have a chance of living responsibly with our feelings, without denying them and paying for this "virtue" with illnesses.

I would be suspicious if a therapist promised me that after treatment (and possibly thanks to forgiveness) I would be free of undesirable feelings like rage, anger, or hatred. What kind of person would I be if I could not react, temporarily at least, to injustice, presumption, evil, or arrogant idiocy with feelings of anger or rage? Would that not be an amputation of my emotional life? If therapy really has helped me, then I should have access to *all* my feelings for the rest of my life, as well as conscious access to my own history as an explanation for the intensity of my responses. This would quickly temper that intensity without having serious physical consequences of the kind caused by the suppression of emotions that have remained unconscious.

In therapy I can learn to understand my feelings rather than condemn them, to regard them as friends and protectors instead of fearing them as something alien that needs to be fought against. Though parents, teachers, or priests may have taught us to practice such self-amputation, we must ultimately realize that it is in fact very dangerous. There can be no doubt that we are then the victims of severe mutilation.

It is not our feelings that make us a danger to ourselves and our environment; it is the dissociation of those feelings caused by our fear of them. It is here that we must seek the reasons for amok killers, for suicide bombers, and for the countless court judges who close their eyes to the real causes of crime, so as to spare the parents of the delinquents and to keep their own histories in the dark.

5

The Wellsprings
of Horror

W HOEVER THEY ARE, and however dreadful their crimes, deep down inside every dictator, mass murderer, and terrorist cowers the humiliated child they once were, a child that has only survived through the complete and utter denial of his or her feelings of helplessness. But this denial of suffering once borne creates an inner void. Very many of these people will never develop a capacity for normal human compassion. Accordingly, they have few if any qualms about destroying human life, neither that of others nor of themselves via the void they carry around within them. Today we can see the damage (lesions) in the brains of abused or neglected children on the computer screen. Articles by brain specialists, including Bruce D. Perry, himself a child psychiatrist, give us the necessary information on this point.

From my vantage, and on the basis of the research I have done on the childhood of ruthless dictators such as Hitler, Stalin, Mao, and Ceauşescu, I see terrorism in general and the terror attacks we hear about almost every day as a macabre but precise demonstration of what millions and millions of children all over the world are subjected to every day in the name of good parenting. And unfortunately society turns a blind eye. All of us have experienced as adults what these children go through. They stand helpless, speechless, and trembling before the unpredictable, incomprehensible, brutal, indescribable violence of their parents, who thus avenge themselves unconsciously for the sufferings of their own childhood, sufferings they have never come to terms with because they have denied their very existence. We only need recall our feelings in response to September 11, 2001, to have some idea of the intensity of those sufferings. All of us were gripped by horror, dread, and fear. But the connections between terrorism and childhood are still hardly recognized. It is time to take the facts seriously.

The statistics (see Olivier Maurel, *La fessée*, Éditions La Plage, 2001) tell us that 90 percent of the people living on this planet are firmly convinced that beating children is all for their own good. As almost all of us have endured the humiliations spawned by this mentality, the cruelty involved is something we have learned to consider normal. But like the Holocaust and other supreme instances of contempt for human life and dignity, terrorism demonstrates the effects of the punitive system in which we have all grown up. Everyone can contemplate the horrors of terrorism on their television screens. But the media pay little attention to the horrors in which children grow up because we have all learned in early childhood to suppress the pain, avert our eyes from the truth, and deny the infinite feeling of helplessness inflicted on a humiliated child.

Contrary to former belief, we do not arrive in this world with a brain fully formed. It develops fully only in the first few years of life. The things, good or bad, done to the child in that period leave lifelong traces. Our brains store the complete physical and emotional—though not mental—memory of everything that has happened to us. If children have no "helping witnesses" to turn to, they will glorify what has been inflicted on them: cruelty, brutality, hypocrisy, ignorance. Children learn by imitation, not from the well-meant words addressed to them in the later stages of life. The mass murderers, serial killers, Mafia bosses, and dictators will inflict on many others—possibly whole nations—the same terror they were exposed to in childhood. And if they have no power themselves, they will actively connive in establishing such a reign of terror.

Unfortunately, most of us prefer not to see these connections, adhering instead to our childhood strategy: denial. But the increase of uninhibited violence all over the world tells us that we cannot afford this self-imposed blindness any longer. We must grow out of the old system geared to punishment, retaliation, and the eradication of evil in others. Of course, we must not neglect our own safety. But we have hardly any other option than to go in active search of different forms of communication than the ones imprinted on us in childhood, a species of communication based on respect rather than potential humiliation.

It is high time to rouse ourselves from our inertia. As adults, we are no longer threatened by the same danger of destruction that many of us were really exposed to in infancy, paralyzing us with fear and driving us to denial. Only in childhood is denial the sole means of survival. As adults, we can learn to stop ignoring the knowledge stored in our bodies because there is real danger in being unable to understand the true motives behind our actions. Instead, the knowledge of our own histories can free us from the instinctive desire to employ futile strategies and remain emotionally blind. Today we have the chance to look around, learn from experience, and devise new, creative solutions for conflicts. Humiliation of others will never be an effective solution in the long term. Instead, it will spawn new violence, both in parenting and in politics. As children, we may not have learned to trust in respectful communication, but it is never too late to make up for that. This learning process seems to me a meaningful and promising alternative to self-deception with the aid of power.

6

Private Mania

THERE ARE VARIOUS motives that repeatedly prompt me to return to the biography of Adolf Hitler. The most important of them is that I know of no other dictator whose childhood and later life are so thoroughly documented. Usually, reliable accounts of the child years of famous or notorious individuals are difficult to come by. The official biographies rarely contain anything of value in this respect. The parents are frequently idealized, but hardly any mention is made of the way they actually treated their children. Most biographers are unaware of the importance of cruelty and maltreatment in childhood. The various biographies of Hitler are no exception, although the material on his early years that I have collected and quoted might have been expected to make a difference in this connection.[1]

My investigations of the roots of perversion, brutality, sadism, and cruelty are all attempts to provide material that may help to prevent such things in the future. But this will only be possible when we have identified and grasped the mechanisms operative in the mindless production of what we generally refer to vaguely as "evil." I know of no other biography better suited to this purpose than that of Adolf Hitler. There are various reasons for this.

1. The accounts by his siblings are congruent. His stepbrother Alois, his half-sister Angela, and his sister Paula are unanimous in their descriptions of the daily beatings meted out to the young Adolf by his father. Such agreement is highly unusual, for we know that even today the siblings of cruelly treated children will normally spare the parents and hardly ever testify to this kind of brutality. But in Hitler's case things are very different, and this is a major exception to the rule. The accounts by his siblings and other witnesses (for example, the domestic servants) and various references in *Mein Kampf* indicate clearly how young Adolf's self-confidence and self-awareness were systematically suffocated. He was never allowed to express an opinion or display his feelings. He suffered vicious lashings on the slightest pretext. He had no idea of what he could do or how he should be to earn the right to exist in this family. When his despair drove him to run away from home at the age of eleven, his father caught him and derided him. What recourse is left to children that are not even granted the right to existence? If there are no "helping witnesses" on hand, the only way out may be an escape into the realms of fantasy, to imagine how one day they will be big and powerful and able to inflict the kind of destruction on others that threatens them now. Constant humiliation of children can cause them as adults to develop delusions of grandeur and avenge themselves on innocent people for the

horrors inflicted on them. This path from humiliation in childhood to adult megalomania is observable in all dictators, though the beginnings of such a "career" are usually left in the dark. I have illustrated the point in connection with Ceauşescu,[2] but Franco, Idi Amin, or Pol Pot would certainly provide just as much evidence of the long-term consequences of the denial of childhood traumas or the private mania typical of dictators.

2. In addition, Hitler's richly documented life history also contains a great deal of material on the childhood of his parents, especially his father's. This customs official so proud of the power he exercised over others and so ready to beat his son black and blue every day was the illegitimate son of a supposedly Jewish merchant and his domestic servant. At the time, such an occurrence was a profound disgrace, not only in the little village of Braunau where it happened, but almost everywhere else as well. Hitler's grandmother received alimony from the merchant for fourteen years. Alois Hitler was adopted by one of the grandmother's relatives, a man who changed his name on various occasions, as the official records disclose. His descent must have been a major blot on the family escutcheon. This traumatic history left its mark on his whole life and dictated his behavior to his son Adolf. It provides important information on the wellsprings of a form of mania that was later to culminate in the establishment of the extermination camps. Naturally, Hitler's mania alone would not have sufficed if he had not been actively assisted by millions of others. Anti-Semitism had always existed in a latent form, but prior to Hitler no one had ever contemplated physically exterminating the Jewish people in its entirety. It was Hitler's very own history that gave this anti-Semitism a dimension it had

never reached before. And it was Hitler's history of childhood humiliation that enabled him to rally all those who had been through similar experiences to his atrocious cause. He had so completely internalized the intimidating postures and attitudes of his sadistic father that his audiences trembled like little children when he ranted and raved in the way his father had done. The sadism the young Adolf had experienced and learned at the hands of his father later conjoined with the latent sadism of millions of others to give him the "legitimation" he required to carry out his appalling schemes with brutal efficiency.

3. The way Hitler's childhood was reflected in the so-called Third Reich can be illustrated by a number of examples.

- Suspicion of Jewish descent became a matter of life and death. Only those who could prove down to the third generation that they had no Jewish forefathers were safe. All others were doomed. At no other period or site in the history of Jewish persecution did such a law exist. Even in the days of the Spanish Inquisition, Jews had a chance of survival if they converted to Christianity. But under Hitler's dictatorship even converted Jews were murdered. There was no refuge for them, just as there had been no refuge for the young Adolf and his father before him. Though this customs official had a reputable job, he could never shake off the "disgrace" of Jewish descent.

- In the Third Reich sadism was declared the supreme principle. In his book *Hitler's Willing Executioners: Ordinary Germans and the Holocaust*,[3] Daniel Goldhagen describes how some people did everything they could to obtain positions that would enable them to torment others. Hitler elevated sadism to the status of a virtue by declaring it right and proper to torture Jews. What are the origins of this pleasure in degrading, humiliating, and tormenting others, the need to act in this way? It is invariably nothing other than the suppressed and denied memories of a child sadistically abused by its parents and later wreaking revenge on others for the horrors thus experienced.

- In the Third Reich Jews were designated as nonpersons, creatures of the lower orders. This devaluation was another attitude Adolf Hitler adopted from his father, who treated him as an inferior being he could deride, mock, and abuse with impunity.

- The insane idea of a world free of Jews can also be traced back to the fate inflicted on Hitler as a child. I can readily imagine that he may have been exposed to scorn and disparagement at school for his father's supposedly Jewish descent, and that there may have been tensions at home for the same reason. As a result, he indulged in fantasies of a life that was very different from his own, a life that was not disfigured by "the Jews." Had he not experienced the cruelty of a "Jew" in the merciless beatings meted out to him by his father? As a result, he entertained the idea that all Jews were cruel and overpowering, just like his father, and for that reason should be destroyed so that the "Aryans" (Adolf himself) could live in peace.

When I point out the connections between a person's childhood experiences and later political phenomena, I frequently encounter major resistance and a striking degree of disconcerted puzzlement. Of course, this kind of thinking is unusual. But anyone taking the trouble to look more closely at the facts will hardly be able to deny the logical progression discernible in the chain of events.

Some readers who have taken that trouble tell me that while they quite see the point of my research on Hitler, the situation we are confronted with today is very different: the danger of terrorism. This is undoubtedly true. But to my mind the underlying problem is very much the same. Terrorism is the product of hatred born of despair, and there is an almost universal refusal to acknowledge that this hatred is not inborn. It originates from a person's childhood, and that means that in principle it is avoidable. If we reject these facts, we are acting very much in the same way as people patiently cleansing river water of chemicals without facing up to the fact that the major chemical plants are dumping this waste in the river every day. It is only logical that a person exposed to violence throughout childhood without "helping witnesses" to turn to and who grows up with a fund of latent hatred should at some point turn into a "time bomb." Once an ideology sanctifies this hatred, those time bombs are bound to explode. The only thing that differs is the enemy. For the Crusaders it was the Infidels; for the Ku Klux Klan the blacks as well as Jews; for the Nazis the Jews, Gypsies, and homosexuals; for the Serbs the Croatians; and so forth. But the motive force behind the slaughter and the desire to kill has always been the urge to avenge the humiliations experienced in childhood and repressed ever since.

People brought up cruelly (and unfortunately that is still the majority) willingly submit to dictators and cheer them on when they supply them with an enemy they can execrate. In democratic states it is by no means unusual for them to elect an egocentric, slovenly exploiter if his attitude reminds them of their fathers. All he needs to do is to assure them that with God's aid his absurd enterprises and plans will turn out well (though, as in the case both of Hitler and Napoleon, they may be motivated by some personal mania or the permanent fear of being unable to live up to their parents' expectations). In their blindness people allow themselves, as allegedly "free" citizens, to be governed and misused by such politicians because they learned this kind of tolerance in childhood. There too they were denied the awareness of how their will, their common sense, and their intuition were beaten into submission.

The ideologies or religions drawn upon to turn people into naïve, unseeing subjects are completely immaterial. As we know, almost any kind of idea can be used to change people abused in childhood into mindless marionettes serving the purposes of the powerholders. Even if the truly exploitative character of these revered and beloved leaders is exposed for what it is after their death or disempowerment, this has hardly any effect on the admiration and unconditional loyalty of their adherents. They symbolize the good father we longed for but never had.

The Crusades, the Inquisition, the Holocaust, and genocide in Rwanda and elsewhere show that abused children will always be waiting for an opportunity to avenge themselves on scapegoats and give uncontrolled vent to all the repressed emotions festering in their hearts, minds, and bodies ever since. This is why I keep coming back to the minutely documented example of Adolf Hitler from which I have learned so much. Many of the ideas I have advanced in the aftermath can be traced back to the initial realizations it gave me about the dynamics of hatred. Above all, it was insight into the atmosphere prevailing during Hitler's childhood that supplied some of the most important arguments. It showed me how disregarded and denied injuries sustained by a child at the time when the brain is in the process of formation can under certain circumstances become a breeding ground for horrors affecting millions of people.

I hope that this thorough knowledge of Hitler's biography will enable other scholars, scientists, and researchers to understand the many crimes that are triggered by this hatred and desire for revenge. We have no comparable material on the childhood experiences of present-day mass murderers and suicide bombers. Of course, the application of this method depends on the extent to which we have faced up to the sufferings of our own childhood years instead of playing them down. Only then is it possible to empathize with the infant sufferings of others. But perhaps the opposite direction is also conceivable. Under certain circumstances, insight into another's sufferings may also make it easier for us to gain emotional access to our own histories.

As we have seen, Hitler's biography is an unending source of enlightenment. But to profit from it fully, we need to have jettisoned the compulsion to idealize our own parents. Then we will realize that in essence the remarks I have been making have very little to do with Hitler himself. The lesson we can learn is that hatred and destructiveness can materialize in very different ways. Whatever ideologies are drawn upon to legitimize them, they spring from one common root. And that root is always the same.

Like Hitler, Joseph Stalin was exposed to incredible brutality as a child and had no helping witness to turn to. He had no idea that it was his bodily memory that drove him to act out his private history of unremitting childhood distress on the colossal stage afforded him by the immensity of the Soviet Union. Stalin was an only child born, like Hitler, after three siblings had died in infancy before him. From the outset he was mercilessly beaten by his irascible father, who was almost invariably the worse for drink. Despite his meteoric career, he was tormented all his life by a persecution mania that prompted him to have millions of innocent people killed. As a child, Stalin had lived in dread of being killed at any moment by his unpredictable father. As an adult, this caused him to live in fear even of his closest associates. But now he had the power to fend off that fear by humiliating others.

Mao was the son of a "strict" teacher who set out to drum obedience and wisdom into him with the aid of severe physical correction. We know all about the "wisdoms" Mao later attempted to instill in the vast population of his country, ostensibly with the best of intentions, but at the price of 35 million deaths. Ceauşescu grew up sharing a room with ten brothers and sisters. His delayed response was to force Romanian women to have children they did not want.[4]

The list of examples is endless. Unfortunately, we refuse to look the facts in the face. But from them we can learn how hatred originates, and if we took that lesson seriously, we would be much less prone to believe that there is nothing we can do about it.

The Roots of Hatred

Why are we so anxious to find innate evil tucked away in our genetic makeup? Quite simply because most of us were beaten when we were small and fear nothing so much as the revival of the pain caused by those humiliations. At the same time, we were told that it was all for our own good, so we learned to suppress that pain. But the memories of those humiliations remained stored away in our brains and bodies. We loved our parents, so we believed them when they told us that smacks and slaps were good for us. Most of us still believe it and go around asserting that children cannot be brought up without blows and the humiliation that goes with them. And then there is no way out of the vicious circle and the denial of the humiliation thus inflicted. The need for revenge, retaliation, and punishment lives on unabated. The rage suppressed in childhood turns into murderous hatred. Religious and ethnic groups are only too willing to supply the ideologies justifying the cultivation and projection of that hatred. Humiliation is a poison that is all but impossible to counteract. It produces new humiliation fueling the proliferation of violence and camouflaging the underlying problems.

To break out of this vicious circle we must face up to our own truth. We were humiliated children, we were the victims of our parents' ignorance, of their unconscious histories, the scars their childhood left on them. But as adults we can break out of that mold. Unlike a child growing up without "helping witnesses," we as adults have healthier alternatives than denial. We can decide in favor of knowledge and awareness, instead of allowing ourselves to be driven by the emotional, unconscious knowledge stored in our bodies and the fear of the truth it instills in us. We may feel immense reluctance about recognizing this activity of our emotional and bodily memory, because the insights it affords us are independent of our conscious minds and are also new and unaccustomed. Above all, this is a species of memory that we have no control over. But awareness of these phenomena can in fact give us better control over them and greater protection against their effects. A mother who gives her child a slap "involuntarily" or "instinctively" will not normally be aware that she only does so because her body and its memories have driven her to do so. (Mothers not beaten as children do not normally hit their children "involuntarily"). But if she is aware of the fact, she can deal with this impulse more effectively; she will have more control over herself and spare both herself and the child the suffering that is bound to result.

Equipped with the knowledge we have at our disposal today, we might gradually espouse different notions and solutions from the ones handed down to us in a thousand-year tradition of violence, punishment, and retribution (supported by weakness, ignorance, and fear). Electing to remain bogged down in these inherited notions is tantamount to a refusal to learn from the facts we have at our disposal. Why is it that in the last two thousand years no representative of the church has modeled his behavior on that of Jesus Christ? Why has the church never spoken out against corporal punishment for little children? The church preaches—and practices—compassion, tolerance, and forgiveness for adults but expressly denies those blessings to children. Why do Christian schools in Africa get up in arms when the government of the Republic of Comoros sets out to prohibit physical correction for pupils? The reason given in the petition opposing this decision is that physical correction for schoolchildren is a religious duty. The only reason there can be for such extreme psychological obscurantism is that the adults involved are immured in a tradition of power, retaliation, and vengeance for denied humiliations that they are unwittingly passing on to the next generation.

If the Bible and the Quran had clearly prohibited cruelty to children, we could look to the future with an easier mind. Unfortunately, however, leading religious authorities obstinately refuse to countenance new and vital information about the dangers this involves for the infant brain. They have not the slightest intention of speaking out in favor of respectful treatment for children and hence for the future of humanity because, like intimidated children and like Luther, Calvin, and many philosophers before and since, they are primarily concerned to protect and elevate the immaculate image of their own mothers. This is the idealized image of a mother who did the right thing when she mercilessly thrashed her children. For all the fine words written about love and charity, they refuse to see how the capacity for love is destroyed in children.

7

Ideal Soldiers:
When Will We
No Longer Need Them?

BEATEN, HUMILIATED, TORMENTED children with no helping witness to turn to for aid frequently develop a serious syndrome in later life. They are ignorant of their own feelings, they even fear them like the plague, and accordingly they are unable to perceive a number of vital connections. As adults, they take out the cruelty they have experienced on innocent people, without noticing it and without accepting responsibility for it because, like their parents before them, they see this as a "redemption" for others. The result is highly irresponsible behavior decked out in spurious legitimacy by any number of different ideologies coupled with unlimited hypocrisy. Especially in an age like ours, when technology appears to know no bounds, this leads directly to inimical and inhuman actions posing a serious threat to the future of our planet.

"We don't want to beat you but we have to in order to banish the evil that you have brought into the world with you." This is what parents believed in Luther's day, and this is how they spoke to their children. Luther told them it was their duty to release their children from the clutches of the devil and to make them into God-fearing little Christians by beating the living daylights out of them. And they believed him. They had no way of knowing that as a child Luther had been ferociously flayed by his mother and that his affirmation of this kind of upbringing was designed to preserve the image of a good and loving mother that he had created with the aid of denial and repression.

Because they believed him, they did not know that instead of exorcising the "devil" in their innocent children, their cruelty was in fact planting the "seeds of evil" in them. The harder and the more often they beat their children, the worse they became, exacerbating the destructiveness of the later adult when those "seeds" came to fruition.

Do present-day parents know better? Many do, but by no means all. Even today, four hundred years later, many of them are confirmed in their ignorance by so-called authorities. It is only the terminology that has changed. We no longer speak of the devil in connection with parenting. It is the "genes" that are to blame. Some media have no qualms about ignoring the history of the last world war and the lessons it teaches us, informing their readers with blithe disregard for all the progress that has been made that crime and mental disorders can be traced back to the genes. This goes hand in hand with advocacy of the hoary old "wisdom" that insists that leniency in youth is harmful and that this is the reason there are so many disturbed adolescents in present-day society.

Does reality not contradict these assertions? Were Hitler, Himmler, and Eichmann treated too indulgently? Ask the advocates of physical correction these questions, and you will not get an answer. The point is that their ideology has no truck with the facts. Instead, it is fueled by these people's own repressed experiences. Here an entirely different kind of logic prevails, the logic of repression, which has no difficulty in dealing with contradictions. Its purpose is not to find out the truth but to preclude the resurgence of old wounds.

Every individual enters this world free of evil intentions, with the strong and unequivocal need to preserve his or her own life, to love and to be loved. But if children encounter not love and truth but hatred and lies, if they are beaten rather than protected, then it must surely be their inalienable right to scream out their protests at such idiocy and evil. This would be the healthy and natural response to the destructive attacks mounted against them by adults. Such protest would salve their mental health, their dignity, self-esteem, integrity, self-awareness, and responsibility.

But beaten, neglected, and abused children are not allowed to defend themselves. All the recourses bestowed on them by nature for the purposes of self-preservation are out of bounds. Such protest might even cost them their lives.

In addition, an organism still in the process of growth has no way of dealing with such overwhelming feelings. In most cases children will accordingly suppress the memory of this trauma and the potent but undesired feelings that go with such injuries: murderous rage, desire for revenge, and the feeling of being threatened by the whole world. For a child without "helping witnesses" the parents *are* the whole world. So it is only too likely that in the child's unconscious brain the desire to destroy that world will materialize as the only prospect of survival.

As all these feelings are repressed, as they are never consciously experienced, as the need for respect, truth, and love have never been adequately articulated, many of these injured children go in search of symbolic satisfaction, for example in the socially acknowledged forms of perversion and crime. Weapons manufacture, the arms trade, and ultimately war are ideal scenes in which they can vent the murderous rage stored in the organism but successfully repressed and never consciously experienced. But this rage is vented on people who have no part in its genesis, while denial and idealization are pressed into service to spare the true culprits.

In warfare everything is permitted that was previously forbidden. The image of an enemy suffices to divert the pent-up hatred and the limitless, unbounded, blind destructive rage of the little child, uncontrolled and uncorrected because never consciously experienced, into permissible channels without those feelings ever needing to penetrate into the conscious mind.

A United States pilot involved in the Gulf War of 1990–91 was once asked what he felt on returning from an air raid. His answer was gratification at having done a good job. "Was that all?" the journalist asked. "What else was I supposed to feel?" the pilot answered with unruffled equanimity. If this man had been allowed to feel, if his feelings had not been frozen for years on end, he might have sympathized with the fear, helplessness, and rage of the people he had been bombarding, he might even have sensed the former helplessness of the small boy exposed to a rain of blows. Then he would have appreciated the connection between humiliation experienced at an early stage and the satisfaction of being able to threaten others with bombs and no longer being a helpless victim. He would no longer have been an ideal soldier, but as a conscious human being he might have been able to help others see through the insanity they were conniving in. He could have contributed to preventing war in future. Wars are tolerated because there are countless people for whom both their own lives and those of others are worthless and execrable, people who have learned to destroy or be destroyed. These people have never been able to develop a love of life because they have never had the opportunity to do so.

Stronger than Weapons

If we do not want to count among their victims, all we can do is to appreciate that this hatred is stronger than any weapons we can conceive of. We must finally understand that this hatred can be resolved if we only know how. What we experience today is the consequence of the repression of our early sufferings, dissociation from our feelings, and the resultant inability to see the connections.

An excellent example of this is the production of poison gas. Who, after all, wanted the Gulf War? The German companies merely wanted to earn money by producing and selling poison gas. This is quite legitimate, is it not? And it is equally legitimate to be impervious to the consequences and never spare a thought for the suffering thus visited on others. Did the German government want poison gas to be manufactured in its country? Not at all. The fact that the honest taxpayers tolerated this is equally legitimate, right? Did no one recall that this was gas for killing people? It was no one's job to think such thoughts. Everyone has his own department, but there is no Department for Useless Thoughts. But what about the Belgian toxicologist Aubin Hendrickx? Did he not inform the United Nations and various governments about the lethal nature of this gas? Why did his representations fall on deaf ears?

Young people of today may ask these questions, aghast. The

answers they receive are always the same: "I had no idea, it wasn't my department, I wasn't responsible, I was acting on instructions." Such responses are chillingly reminiscent of similar statements in the postwar period. The Nazis exterminated whole peoples with poison gas, calling it a "clean" solution because millions of people were killed without bloodshed. The sons who never summoned up the courage to look their fathers' atrocities in the face are later participating in a potential revival of those atrocities because they never seriously questioned them in the first place. If they had, they would have realized the atrocity of those atrocities and would then have been incapable of perpetuating them.

Here we see the logic of repression at work. I refuse to acknowledge what my parents did to me and others, I forgive them blindly, I prefer not to look any closer, not to condemn them, not to question them. They remain inviolate because they are my parents. Since my system (my body) knows what happened, although I have no conscious memory of it as long as my feelings are blocked off, I feel the urge to repeat the crimes perpetrated on me (destruction of life) without noticing it. In the abuse of my own children, in the cruel battle against people I have declared my enemies, in the destruction of life wherever it flourishes, I can erect a monument to my parents and prove my undying loyalty to them. Millions of degraded and humiliated children unable to defend themselves against the destructive attacks on their personal integrity are reminded by war of the more or less completely repressed history of the threats they were exposed to. They feel upset and confused. But as they usually have no access to those early memories and the feelings that go with them, they cannot appreciate them for what they are. To escape from their own painful histories, they have recourse to the methods they learned as children: destroy or be destroyed, but stay blind at all costs. In their blindness they seek escape from something that already happened long ago.

To spare themselves the story of the painful humiliations passed off on them as tokens of love, men go to prostitutes, pay them for lashings, and persuade themselves, much as their parents persuaded them all those years ago, that they are actually benefiting from this tragic situation (the loss of dignity and inner orientation). To consign the memory of their own fathers' sexual abuse to oblivion, some women become prostitutes and subject themselves to further humiliation in line with the old illusion that constantly changing partners and the malleability of men will give them something akin to power. The S/M industry and the various flagellation clubs thrive on this burning desire (both of men and women) to inter the history of their childhood once and for all with the help of new, but basically very similar, scenarios. However, this plan is doomed to misfire, and they constantly have to explore new avenues so as not to have to face up to the truth of their own childhood. Alcohol and drug excesses suggest themselves, but the price is high.

Wars, on the other hand, offer us free of charge—though not without cost in the long run—a tremendous scenario of a similar kind. They provide an ideal opportunity to rid ourselves of the emotional pressure that has dogged us since childhood, either by destroying or being destroyed. Recently, a television program showed footage of an elite unit of the United States Army undergoing training in how to withstand torture in captivity. This brutal training had much in common with the practices of the nineteenth-century German "educator" Dr. Daniel Moritz Schreber, who asserted that the torments he inflicted on children were designed to "harden" them and were hence all for their own good.

He recommended them as a universal parenting strategy. The fact that, just like the officers in charge of the elite unit, he was gratifying his own sadistic urges in the process escaped the notice of his victims. That unit included women, and participation was entirely voluntary.

Knowing, as we do, from inquiries into the childhood histories of the Green Berets that virtually all volunteers taking part in the Vietnam War were subjected to brutal training methods designed to instill unconditional obedience in them, very much like the Nazi criminals, we no longer have to ask ourselves why people volunteer to let themselves be treated in such an absurdly sadistic manner. All that is needed is to tell them, as they were told in childhood, that this will make them impervious to later tortures because they have learned to be tough, unfeeling, and "cold-blooded." If these sons and daughters had access to their own histories, they would find much more meaningful and productive ways of preserving themselves and the world from real dangers. Unlike children, adults are unlikely to actually die from the indignation and pain caused by the sufferings inflicted on them. They have no reason to resign themselves to blindness and the constant flight from something that happened a long time ago. There are ways of achieving access to our repressed histories.

Even the most effective weapons will never halt the production of new and even more terrible weapons, nor will they do away with destructive hatred as long as this hatred is deflected onto substitutes, disguised by ideology, and left unresolved in its original context. If we want to protect life on this planet, then we must challenge this dangerous blindness wherever we encounter it and above all in ourselves.

People who know about their own histories will not sacrifice themselves for other people's attempts to settle old scores and escape from their own past. They will find other and much better ways of settling conflicts than saber-rattling and the destruction of life. Nor will they feel the need to sacrifice others to escape their own truth. They will be fully familiar with it. There is no alternative to the truth, to the confrontation with our individual and collective histories. Knowledge of that truth is the only thing that can protect us from perfect self-destruction.

8

Sheer Sadism

MANY PEOPLE WORLDWIDE were horrified at the perversions practiced on Iraqi captives by American soldiers during the first years of the Iraq War. But I have rarely experienced such indignation in response to sadistic practices exercised on children, for example in American and British schools. The reason is that such practices have always been classified as part of their education. Brutality inflicted on adults is (quite rightly) branded as scandalous. The world is frequently astonished that such brutality should even raise its ugly head among Americans, who have successfully persuaded the international public that they are the guardians of global peace. But all this is susceptible of explanation, though this explanation is hardly ever advanced.

Accordingly, it is certainly a good thing that light has finally been cast on the situation, that the lie has been exploded by the media. This lie runs as follows: We are a civilized, freedom-loving nation, and we bring democracy and independence to the remotest corners of the earth. It was with this motto on its banners that the United States invaded Iraq, causing immense devastation while still insisting that it was importing cultural values. Now it transpires that the well-drilled, smartly dressed soldiers not only had bombs and rockets in tow but also a huge arsenal of pent-up rage, invisible for all, including themselves, carefully concealed but none the less dangerous for that.

One asks oneself where this suppressed rage comes from, this desire to torment, mock, and abuse helpless captives. What are these apparently doughty soldiers avenging themselves for? And where did they learn such behavior? The same place as everyone else learns it: first as small children in the family, where they were taught to obey with the help of physical abuse; then at school, where they were exposed as defenseless victims to the sadism of some of their teachers; and finally during their military training, when they were treated like dirt by their superior officers with a view to instilling in them the questionable ability to put up with anything and toughening them up.

Desire for revenge does not come from nowhere. Its origins are to be found in the first years of life, when children are forced to suffer in silence as they are cruelly abused in the name of good parenting. The torture methods are learned first from the parents, later from teachers and superiors. Yet many people expect this systematic instruction by example in the destruction of others to have no evil consequences, as if children were containers that can be emptied from time to time. But the human brain is not a container. The things we learn early on in life are more or less irreversible. This is the lesson of the incidents in Iraq.

In *The Body Never Lies*, I point out that in twenty-two states of the U.S., children and adolescents at school are legally beaten, humiliated, frequently exposed to sadistic treatment and hence to real-life torture.* But this behavior is not reckoned to be torture because it goes by the name of education, discipline, or leadership. The religions endorse these practices. No one raises their voice in protest, except in a few Web sites on the Internet. By contrast, the Internet is full of advertisements offering whips and other devices for the corporal punishment of small children so that they can become God-fearing individuals of the kind the Good Lord needs and can love. The scandal in Iraq indicates what actually becomes of these children, what kind of adults they grow into. These soldiers are the fruits of an upbringing based on violence, spite, and indeed perversion.

The media quote psychology experts insisting that the brutality displayed by these American soldiers is a product of wartime stress or commands from their superior officers. It is certainly true that the soldiers in Iraq were encouraged in their perverted behavior by instructions from their officers. But the ground had already been laid for this willingness to torture others. It is definitely true that a state of war will trigger aggression, but that aggression must have been present in a latent form beforehand. No individual who has been brought up in a nonviolent manner at home or at school could ever mock and maltreat defenseless captives. It would be impossible. We know from the history of the Second World War that, if they had grown up without violence inflicted on them, drafted soldiers were capable of showing a human face, even in the extremely stressful situation that warfare represents. We also

*Corporal punishment is currently legal in twenty-one U.S. states.

know from many accounts of camp life and armed hostilities that even such extreme stress did not necessarily turn human beings into perverts.

Perversion has a long, obscure history invariably rooted in childhood. The fact that these stories normally remain hidden from society is by no means surprising. All too many people once cowed into obedience by violence have reason enough not to be reminded of their childhood sufferings and never to let the suppressed facts see the light of day. Instead, they prefer to have themselves lashed in S/M clubs and insist that they enjoy the experience instead of asking themselves why they are prepared to submit to such perversions. In our society the cult of the unconscious still appears to flourish untrammeled. It is not true that there is a "wild beast in all of us," as is so often unthinkingly asserted. That beast only lurks in people who were treated in a perverted manner in their childhood and yet stoutly deny the fact. They seek and find scapegoats for their unconscious vengeance, or destroy themselves with drugs and other substances so as to drown out awareness of the deeds perpetrated on them. For the child this pain would have been unbearable. But adults can bear it, and thanks to their own awareness they can banish the "beast" forever.

9

The Tragedy of Jessica

I T DID NOT happen during the war, nor in the so-called Third
World. It happened in the middle of Europe, in one of its
most civilized countries. In 2005 a small girl by the name of
Jessica was starved to death by her parents in the German city
of Hamburg. They looked on impassively as the child attempted
to stave off the pangs of hunger by eating her own hair or bits of
material she had bitten out of the mattress. At the same time,
they indulged themselves to the hilt, washed their food down with
lashings of alcohol, enjoyed their meals, and did nothing to save
their daughter's life.

Understandably, most people believe that there can be no explanation for this fathomless hatred for a child of one's own. Such
extreme cruelty is regarded by the public at large as entirely incomprehensible. Journalists are at a loss to identify the motives behind
such an "unprecedented" crime. But the really astonishing thing is

6

that the so-called experts, medical and psychological, agree that this case is unprecedented, although almost every day there are reports of perverted child abuse in the newspapers. Inquiries into the causes of such behavior, however, are rare. One can hardly avoid the impression that there is some tacit agreement preventing people from asking the simple question "Why?"

This taboo manifests itself clearly in the expert opinions on such cases. Their authors make no mention of something that they must be fully aware of, namely that the cruelty displayed by such criminals is produced in their childhood, at a time before their brains are fully formed. Is it conceivable that they may not in fact know this? In Jessica's case, it is quite clear, and it indicates the consequences that everyday mistreatment like slaps and childhood neglect can have at a later stage.

A woman who went to school with Jessica's mother, Marlies, described her as highly disturbed in her childhood. She stuttered, dribbled, trembled, and invariably came to school in a state of fear and distress. Marlies herself mentioned a number of significant details, for example that her mother had watched her being sexually molested by her great-uncle and had never intervened. A female relative reported that the six-year-old child had been forced to watch pornographic movies with her parents in their bed. There can be no doubt that Marlies had not only experienced a major trauma that the experts had allegedly been unable to identify; but throughout her childhood she had been subjected to extreme cruelty, the memories of which she attempted to keep at bay with an unfeeling attitude. Ultimately, however, she avenged herself on her little daughter Jessica for the hell she had been through as a child. In saying this I am not denying that she committed a crime. The crime is heinous in the extreme. Like all children, Marlies loved her mother. But she had never been able to defend herself against her, and all the pent-up rage at her mother that she never consciously felt was discharged on the little girl, whose slow death she enjoyed with the same sadism that her own mother had displayed in the face of her sufferings. She quite simply tormented Jessica for what her mother had done to her. Marlies's partner reported that she had regarded Jessica's neglect as a "defense measure." This term outlines the situation very accurately. Many mothers only hit back at their own children for the wrongs done to them when they were young. However, Marlies is of course guilty, and she must be punished.

The confusing statements made by experts camouflaging or even denying the causes of such crimes suggest that they are hardly aware of the huge responsibility they bear. A psychiatrist, professor, or medical expert is an authority. What effect will his statements have if he calmly and confidently declares that he does not believe in any traumatic causes of such crimes, as if he were stating his own personal creed rather than facing up to the unassailable evidence?

All we need to do is distinguish between the facts and causes on the one hand, and the question of guilt on the other. A mother who kills her child is definitely guilty because she had a choice. As a child, she was a helpless victim; as an adult this is no longer the case. Here an expert could cast light on the subject, providing enlightenment and helping to prevent future crimes of a similar nature. He could inform the court and the public of how such extreme cruelty repeatedly comes about. While neglecting to provide the courts, the media, and the public with such information and thoroughly confusing them in the process is not a punishable crime, it is certainly a serious failure.

The cruelty of individuals is not something imposed on them by some mysterious agency but by their parents and other people involved in their upbringing. It *takes shape* in the brain of a child exposed to cruelty. This is an established fact from which we cannot avert our eyes, and it should be part of the ABCs of forensic psychiatry. It must no longer be concealed or played down if we want to prevent infanticide and other crimes in future.

The tragedy of Jessica can help parents who believe that slapping their children is justified and harmless to understand their behavior and do something to change it. For that, they require the assistance of courageous, responsible experts, psychiatrists, and reporters.

The horror caused by Jessica's appalling death might have opened some people's eyes and prompted them to ask what it is that so often makes parents hate and abuse their children. As far as I know, little has been done in public debates to confront young parents with these issues. But perhaps it is not too late. Young parents still have the chance to learn a great deal about the production of violence if they are assisted in this process by serious and well-informed experts. This is urgently necessary. The tragedy of Jessica is not an isolated case; it is merely the tip of the iceberg.

III

~

THERAPY: RESOLVING THE CONSEQUENCES OF EARLY CRUELTY

10

The Longest Journey, or What Can We Expect from Psychotherapy?

THE LONGEST JOURNEY of my life was the journey to my own self. I do not know whether I am an exception in this connection, or whether there are other people who have experienced the same thing. It is certainly not a universal experience: fortunately, there are people who from birth were lucky enough to be accepted by their parents for what they were, with all their feelings and needs. Right from the outset these people had unrestricted access to those feelings and needs. They did not have to deny them, nor did they have to embark on long journeys to track something down that was withheld from them when they needed it most.

My experience was different. It has taken me almost all my life to allow myself to be what I am and to listen to what my inner self is telling me, more and more directly, without waiting for permission from others or currying approval from people who symbolize my parents.

I am frequently asked what I understand by successful therapy. I have in fact answered this question indirectly in many of my books. But after this brief introduction perhaps I can put it more simply. Successful therapy should shorten this long journey. It should liberate us from our ingrained adaptation strategies and help us learn to trust our own feelings, something our parents have made difficult, if not impossible, to achieve. Many people are never able to set out on this path because it was prohibited from the outset and thus became a source of fear.

The wide range of self-help books on nonviolent communication, including the valuable and wise advice given by Thomas Gordon and Marshall B. Rosenberg, are undoubtedly effective if they are consulted by people who, in their childhood, were able to display their feelings without fear of rebuke and grew up in the company of adults who served them as a model for being at one with themselves. But at a later stage children with serious impairments to their identity do not know what they feel and what they really need. They have to find this out in therapy, repeatedly applying what they have learned to new experiences and thus achieving the security that tells them they are not mistaken. As children of emotionally immature or confused parents, they were forced to believe that their feelings and needs were wrong. If they had been right, so they believe, then their parents would not have refused to communicate with them.

My belief is that no therapy can fulfill the wish that many people probably harbor: the wish to be able, at long last, to solve all the problems they have been painfully confronted with so far. This is impossible because life repeatedly confronts us with new problems that can reawaken the memories stored away in our bodies. But therapy should open up access to our own feelings: the wounded child must be allowed to speak, and the adult must learn to understand and engage with what that child is trying to say. If the therapist is a genuine "enlightened witness," as opposed to a would-be educator, then the client will have learned to admit his or her emotions, to understand their intensity, and to transform them into conscious feelings that leave new traces of memory. Of course, like any other individual, the former client will need friends with whom to share worries, problems, and questions. But communication will take on a more mature form, free of any kind of exploitation, because both sides have seen through the exploitation experienced in childhood.

The emotional understanding of the child I once was gives me a clearer conception of the biography of that child. Accordingly, it will give me a different kind of access to my own self. It will also give me the strength to deal with present-day problems more rationally and effectively than before. We can hardly expect to be spared any kind of encounter with pain or distressing experience. That is something that only happens in fairy tales. But if I am no longer a mystery to myself, then I can act and reflect consciously; I can give my feelings the room they need to develop. This is because I understand them. And once I understand them, they will no longer cause me as much fear as they once did. This sets things in motion; it gives us a resource that we can draw upon if and when depression or physical symptoms reassert themselves. We know that these physical or mental states are an announcement of something, that they are perhaps trying to bring a suppressed feeling to the surface. And then we can try to admit to that feeling.

As the journey to ourselves is a lifelong journey, its end will not coincide with the end of therapy. But successful therapy should have helped us to discover and perceive our own genuine needs and to learn to satisfy them. This is precisely what individuals wounded in early childhood have never been able to do. So even after therapy the point at issue is still that of satisfying needs, needs that now assert themselves much more strongly and clearly than they did before. The satisfaction of those needs can then take place in a way that accords with the individual in question and does no one else any harm.

We may not always be able to obliterate the traces left by abusive parenting. But once they have been consciously perceived for what they are, they can be used constructively, actively, and creatively, instead of being merely suffered in a passive and self-destructive manner. For example, people only able to survive the early years of life by serving their parents can, as conscious adults, desist from sacrificing their needs in the service of others, as they were forced to do in childhood. They can look for ways of applying the skills they acquired at this early stage to understanding and helping others in such a way that their own needs are not neglected in the process. They may perhaps become therapists themselves and thus satisfy their own curiosity. If they do, they will not practice that profession in order to prove their own power to themselves. Once they have consciously experienced the impotence of their childhood, they will no longer need such proofs.

These people can then become enlightened witnesses, assisting their clients by taking their part and siding with them. This needs to take place in a space that is free of moral pressure, a space where the clients (often for the first time in their lives) can experience what it is like to be aware of their own selves. The therapist will be readily able to place such a space at the clients' disposal if he or she has been through the same experience. The time will have come to cast aside the crutches of morality or professional training (forgiveness, "positive thinking," etc.). These are now superfluous because therapists of this kind will know that both they and their clients have healthy legs they can stand on. Once they are prepared to look their childhood in the face, neither of them will need those crutches any longer.

11

Taking It Personally:
Indignation as
a Vehicle of Therapy

THERE IS NO shortage of books and articles informing us about horrific deeds and circumstances (cruelty to animals, exploitation of nature, torture, despotism, etc.), and it is only natural that we should respond to such accounts with strong feelings. The reaction displayed by a large majority of the thinking and feeling population is one of indignation. But there is an exception to this rule. To a striking degree, reports on the physical abuse of children in the form of spankings or beatings meet with almost total indifference because most people are unaware of the fact that violence is learned by example in the early stages of our lives. But what explanation is there for such ignorance? After all, this knowledge is not a closely guarded secret. At least educated people like teachers, priests, lawyers, or politicians must surely have been confronted with the facts of the matter at some point. Reports on cruelty to children have been common knowledge for at least thirty years, yet there are still no signs of revulsion and horror at this ruthless exploitation of the helpless situation children find themselves in. Cruelty of this kind serves one single purpose: the discharge of the feelings of hatred pent up in adults, parents, and so-called caregivers. But what do we say when we hear a child has been beaten? "So what? That's quite normal, isn't it?" In the last thirty years or so, some people have been raising their voices and insisting that it is in fact anything but normal, that it is both dangerous and ethically unconscionable. But these people are still a small minority. In the 1970s, Sweden passed a law expressly prohibiting the exercise of violence on children. Unfortunately, only 17 states of the 192 members of the United Nations have followed the Swedish example in the interim. We know beyond doubt that by hitting our children we are bringing them up to be the violent parents of the future. But there is no public outcry. Instead, we imperturbably go on cultivating what we claim to be trying to stamp out: torture, war, genocide. We actively connive in the production of tomorrow's violence, tomorrow's illnesses. In each and every case there is incontrovertible evidence that these acts of violence can be traced back to a history of repeated humiliation.[1]

Time and again, I ask myself why it is so difficult to communicate this knowledge, why the perfectly normal response—horror and indignation—fails to materialize when the question at issue is cruelty to small children. What this indicates is that most of us were mistreated as children and had to learn to deny this fact at a very early stage in order to survive. We were forced to believe that we were humiliated and tormented "for our own good." If the brain stores this aberrant information at a very early stage, then the message it conveys will normally retain its effect throughout our lives. It causes persistent mental blockades. In therapy such biases may be resolved. But most people are not prepared to abandon mental blockades of this kind. Instead, they chant this perverse litany: "My parents did their best to bring me up properly, I was a difficult child, and I needed strict discipline." How can people who have been brought up to believe this conceivably feel indignation about cruelty to children? Ever since their own childhood they have been dissociated from their true feelings, from the pain caused by humiliation and torment. To feel their indignation they would need to get back in touch with that childhood pain. And who will want to do that?

Accordingly, this pain very frequently remains locked up behind iron doors in the basement of their souls. And Heaven help anyone who starts battering on those doors! Depression, prescription abuse, drugs, even death—anything is better than being reminded of the torture they went through in the past. So they give it a fine-sounding name—"upbringing"—because that way they can avoid having to feel the pain. As long as they deny the fact that they were childhood victims, these people are incapable of indignation. Only very few face up to the grim facts of their early lives, and if they do so, it frequently makes them feel isolated. For they live in a society where many open-minded individuals feel genuine disgust and indignation at injustices like child labor in Asia but not at the injustice they were themselves exposed to when they were children. This victimization took place when they were too young to be capable of independent thought and accordingly adopted their parents' opinion that they were being tortured for their own good. They espoused this opinion because it enabled them to cultivate loyalty to, and love of, their parents.

While our own biographies may help us to realize why we

are unable to feel indignation at the abuse so many children are exposed to, this inability actively impedes our access to the understanding of a whole range of phenomena. We can illustrate this with reference to some of the problems afflicting present-day society. In the following I have chosen three such problematic issues to indicate how the ability to feel indignation and to resolve our mental paralysis might help us not only to extend our knowledge but also to provide effective remedies and preventive measures where they are urgently needed. These issues are (a) the traditional view of delinquency, (b) the tradition of child abuse in families, and (c) the neutrality principle imposed on psychotherapists.

Mass Murderers and Serial Killers

Both in forensic psychiatry and in psychoanalytic circles, we constantly hear it said that the abominable deeds perpetrated by mass murderers can hardly be the fruits of childhood abuse because some of these killers come neither from broken homes nor from families with an appreciable history of violence. However, if we take the trouble to inquire more closely into their parents' upbringing methods, we are invariably confronted with horrors that are almost as execrable as the crimes committed by the killers themselves. Indeed, as these perversions were visited upon children— for years on end—what we usually refer to as corporal punishment fully deserves to be branded as murder—murder of the soul. As the book *Base Instincts: What Makes Killers Kill?* by Jonathan Pincus demonstrates, (cf. Thomas Gruner's article "Frenzy" on my Web site, www.alice-miller.com) it is by no means difficult to elicit details about parental cruelty from murderers because they themselves hardly ever consider them to be evidence of perversion.

They see them as instances of a perfectly normal upbringing. Like almost all people abused in childhood, these killers are fond of their parents and prepared to go to any lengths to shield them from blame and accusation. Normally, the psychiatrist interviewing such a criminal will adopt this judgment (if he himself has never called his own parents into question) and arrive at the conclusion that for some mysterious reason the serial killer opposite him must have come into the world with destructive genes provoking him to commit his terrible crimes.

I once saw a television report on the increase of juvenile delinquency in our society. The reporter did all he could to understand the motives of the young criminals, interviewing public prosecutors, police officials, and prison governors in his bid to find out more about the causes. Without exception, they all asserted that they had been unable to identify any motives for the murders committed or the serious injuries inflicted on the victims. They also noted that this was typical for the youth of today. The only causes cited for the extreme arousal involved were alcohol or drugs. But there was no inquiry into what had prompted these people to take drugs in the first place. None of the officials questioned gave any sign of awareness of the fact that since their childhood these youngsters had been nursing feelings of revenge.

In twenty years of service a prison warden fully familiar with all the problems posed by an institution of this kind had obviously never given any thought to the question of how juvenile criminals had grown up and who had sown the seeds of violence in their souls. It had never struck him that almost all the crime records reported that the delinquent in question had flown into an uncontrollable rage when he felt offended, humiliated, or disgraced. As a child, he was unable to respond to humiliation. Now he can. The inevitability of subsequent capture and imprisonment is all part of his compulsive desire for punishment, because deep down he has always put the blame for not being loved on himself. This is what he has been told for as long as he can remember.

As a humiliated child, he was never able to learn how to express his anger in words without being punished for it. So instead he immediately resorts to violence, just as his parents did. His brain learned this lesson at a very early stage, and it takes effect immediately when he feels his personal dignity is under attack. But leveling accusations at the assailants who drummed that lesson into him when he was small is taboo. The result is that, after serving their sentences, more than half of the convicted delinquents repeat their crimes and end up back in prison.

In his book *Transforming Aggression*,[2] the analyst Frank M. Lachmann devotes an entire chapter to serial killers. His conclusion is that these people are completely beyond the reach of any kind of empathy. He distinguishes between "guilty" (Freud's Oedipus) and "tragic" (Heinz Kohut) figures, the latter being those who spent their childhood in an unresponsive environment. Psychoanalysts can feel empathy for both, says Lachmann. But for him serial killers and, say, Hitler's henchmen make up a category that must *necessarily* defy our attempts at understanding. These criminals represent evil in its purest form. (Once again, let me point out that my concern here is not to condone the crimes of adult sadists but to understand the sufferings of the children they once were).

So what about terrorist attacks, or instances of genocide as in Rwanda, former Yugoslavia, and so many other places in the world? Can we imagine people wanting to blow themselves sky-high if they were loved, protected, and respected as children? I refuse to accept the idea that people capable of such abominable deeds should be regarded as incarnations of pure evil, thus relieving us of any attempt to identify the roots of this compulsive destructiveness in their biographies. These roots are readily discernible once we open our eyes to the fact that, horrific as the crimes of these adults may be, they are no more appalling than the tortures these criminals were exposed to as children. Then, suddenly, the apparent mystery is solved. We realize that there is not one single mass murderer or serial killer who as a child was not the victim of all kinds of humiliations and psychic murder. But to see that, we need the capacity for indignation that normally lapses into abeyance when we think and talk about childhood. Lachmann's book is an indication that, ultimately, both psychoanalysts and psychiatrists normally shy away from this perspective on childhood suffering. Society pays a very high price for such blindness. If we could help the former victims to give up their indulgence; to rebel against the deeds of their parents, this might suffice to free them of their compulsion to unconsciously reenact their own brutal histories over and over again.

Child Mistreatment: A Family Tradition

Once we have identified the dynamics of compulsive repetition, we will find it in all families where children are mistreated. Frequently, the kind of abuse exercised on children has a long history. The same patterns of humiliation, neglect, exertion of power, and sadism can often be traced back over several generations. To evade the horror this involves, we keep on dreaming up new theories. Some psychologists suggest that the sufferings of their clients derive not from their own childhood but from the histories and problems of distant ancestors that they attempt to resolve with their illnesses.

Such theories have a palliative effect. They save us from having to imagine the sheer hell these clients went through in their youth, and they spare us indignation. But much like the genetic fallacy, this is in fact nothing other than an attempt to escape the painful reality of the matter. Yet many intellectuals believe implicitly and unhesitatingly in such explanations. They subscribe to the notion of intrinsic evil to spare themselves the pain involved in admitting that, whatever justifications may be trotted out to disguise such violence, the real reason why numerous parents torment their children is unconscious hatred. But this is the truth. And once we decide to look it in the face, there are real benefits to be gained from that decision. It enables us to forsake the medieval belief in the devil ("rogue genes"). The chain of violence is shown up for what it is, and we realize that we can do something to break that chain.

Sadistic parents do not fall from the skies. They were treated just as sadistically in their childhood, there is no doubt about that. To assert the opposite is to evade the simple fact that in the formative years of their lives tormented children suffer not only one death, like a murderer's victim, but countless psychic deaths and tortures at the hands of the people they are dependent on and cannot find a substitute for.

It is hard for us to imagine such sadism, although we are only sixty years away from the demise of the Nazi regime, a time when millions were intentionally starved and left to face certain death. But neither then, nor later, nor today has there been any inquiry into the question of how people *become* so sadistic. How were they brought up, how were they deprived of the capacity to rebel against such wrongs, to recognize their parents' cruelty, to defend themselves against it? Instead, they were taught to approve their parents' sadism in all its forms. And this succeeded so completely because children want to love their parents and prefer not to look the truth in the face. The truth is too awful for these children to bear, so they avert their eyes. But the body remembers everything, and as adults those children unconsciously and automatically rehearse their parents' sadism on their own children, on their subjects or employees, on everyone dependent on them. They do not know that they are doing to others precisely what their parents did to them when they were in a state of complete and utter dependence. Some may suspect the fact and seek therapeutic aid. But what do they find there?

Therapy: Neutrality versus Partiality

When I was in training to become a psychoanalyst, a great deal of importance was attached to the analyst's neutrality. This was one of the basic rules considered since Freud to be self-evident and required to be strictly observed at all times. At that point I had no idea that there was any connection between this stricture and the compulsion to protect the patient's parents from any kind of blame. My colleagues seemed to have no difficulty maintaining their neutrality; they appeared to have no interest in empathizing with the torments suffered by a beaten and humiliated child exposed to incestuous exploitation. Perhaps some of them had been the victims of such cruelty. But in their training they were themselves treated with the neutrality demanded by Freud, so they had no opportunity of discovering the pain they had been denying all along. To be able to break with that denial, they would have needed not a neutral therapist but a partial one, someone who sided unequivocally with the tormented child and displayed indignation at the wrongs done to that child *before* the client is capable of doing so. The point is that at the outset of therapy most clients do not feel any indignation. Though they recount facts that invite revulsion and indignation, they have no desire for rebellion, not only because they are dissociated from their feelings, but because they do not know that parents can be any different.

My experience has repeatedly shown me that my genuine indignation at what clients have been through in their childhood is an important vehicle of therapy. This becomes especially apparent in group therapy. Individual members of the group may tell us calmly, possibly even with a smile, that they were locked in a dark cellar for hours if they dared to contradict their parents. This will arouse a murmur of horror among the other members. But the person telling the story is not yet capable of such feelings, they have no basis for comparisons. For them this treatment is normal.

I have also encountered people who spent years in primal therapy and who had no difficulty in weeping over the sufferings they had been through in their childhood. But they were still far from feeling any indignation at the incestuous exploitation or the perverted ritual beatings they had suffered at the hands of their parents. They believed that such inflictions are a normal part of any childhood and that the simple rediscovery of their former feelings would heal them. But this is not always the case, and certainly not if the strong attachment to their unconscious parents and the expectations they have of them continue to subsist. I believe that this attachment and these expectations cannot be resolved as long as the therapist remains neutral. This has struck me in my discussions with therapists working quite correctly with their clients on access to their emotions but still subject to the idealization of their own parents. They could only help their clients when they had been encouraged to admit their own feelings and consequently to express the indignation aroused in them, as therapists, by the perversions inflicted on the clients by their parents.

The effect of this is frequently very striking. It is like clearing away a dam that has been blocking the course of a river. Sometimes the therapist's indignation will quickly release a veritable avalanche of indignation in the client. But this is not always the case. Some clients need weeks, months, even years before this happens. But the open display of indignation on the part of the therapist as witness ultimately sets off a process of liberation that has previously been impeded by the moral standards upheld by society. This unleashing of emotion is due to the free and committed attitude of a therapist able to show the former child that it is *legitimate* to be scandalized at the behavior of one's parents, that *every sentient individual would be scandalized, with the sole exception of those who have actually been tormented as children.*

My remarks on this point may be understood as an attempt on my part to write a prescription for therapists, advising them to develop feelings of indignation so as to help their clients achieve this breakthrough. But that would be a major misunderstanding. I cannot advise someone to have feelings they do not have, and no one can possibly follow such advice. But I assume that there are therapists who are sincerely indignant when they hear of the scandalous behavior of their clients' parents. It is entirely possible that some of them believe that they should not give expression to this indignation because in their training they have been told that this must be avoided at all costs. From Freud's school of thought they may even have learned to regard their feelings as "counter-transference," i.e., as a mere "personal" reaction to their clients' feelings. In this way they have accustomed themselves to avoiding the perception and expression of their own feelings, their simple and eminently understandable response to cruelty.

In such therapy, clients remain trapped in their infant fear. They do not dare to impart their liberating emotions, to experience their anger and indignation as a normal reaction to cruelty and perversion. Accordingly, therapists should be encouraged to trust to their own feelings. Instead of misinterpreting them as instances of countertransference, they should take them seriously, own up to them, and articulate them. This will make it easier for them to avow their indignation because they were not the children of these parents and, unlike their clients, are in a better position to avoid assessing certain kinds of perversion as normal behavior. Therapists can readily check up on the truth of these statements. On no account should they make use of anything that does not square with their authentic feelings or convince them on the basis of their own experience.

The general tendency to evade feelings of indignation is understandable because this feeling can easily spark off a perception of childlike impotence and memories of a time when some of us were hopelessly exposed to the sadism of adults and unable to defend ourselves. It is understandable that we should prefer not to hear about these things and to regard people who engage in such practices as monsters. But as we are increasingly confronted with terrorist violence, we cannot afford to demonize perversion and close our eyes to the way in which sadism is engendered in the first place. If we do not learn to understand the connections and prevent parents from the exercise of their perverted upbringing rituals, then humanity is ultimately doomed to be wiped out by its own dangerous ignorance.

12

Misleading Information

I N A P R O G R A M broadcast on French television (France 3) in March 2004, a number of people who had been victims of sexual abuse in their childhood were given an opportunity to tell their stories. Most of them had come to terms with this abuse in a variety of different therapies, or at least asserted that this was the case. The facts they referred to were shattering. In most cases it was not the parents who had perpetrated these acts of abuse on the children but people from outside the family, pedophiliac priests, teachers, friends of the family. Accordingly, the blame relating to the parents was indirect. At least they had not committed these deeds themselves. But there can be little doubt that they made them possible by averting their eyes. Most of the victims expressed disappointment at their parents' attitude, and this is in itself a major step forward in comparison with the way in which most programs on this subject do their best to play down or cover up the matter.

But here again it was the psychological expert who did everything he could to camouflage the truth. Whereas the legal expert gave a truthful account of the concealment practiced by the courts, the child psychiatrist taking part attempted to contextualize the significance of the facts presented by the victims and even to turn them inside out. He was at pains to focus on the role of infant fantasy, thus chiming in with the Freudian tradition. The former victims would have none of this. But he even went a stage further. After hearing about the damage child abuse had done to the subsequent lives of the victims, driving them to drug dependence, delinquency, and severe illness, he said quite calmly and reassuringly: "Luckily, most victims do not turn into perpetrators themselves, they do not take the experience of abuse out on their own children. Probably less than 10 percent actually do that, the other 90 percent become wonderful parents."

This statement by a child psychiatrist who ought to have certain knowledge of the truth from his own practice, that is if he were only to admit it, was extremely shocking. The question that posed itself was what statistical basis this man had for his assertions. In reality, the opposite is the case, hardly 10 percent manage to evade the danger of repetition, and only if they achieve conscious awareness of their childhood sufferings. Most parents beaten in early life beat their own children and pretend that it is all for their own good. Many of them abuse their children and insist that in this way they are giving them love, just as they heard the same assertions from their parents and others involved in their upbringing. Others cannot prevent themselves from beating their children even when they know in principle it is wrong. How can a child psychiatrist not know that? I believe that what prevents him from facing these facts is the fear of discovering his own denied and repressed history and of feeling the pain it caused him. This is compounded with another fear, that of standing alone if he speaks out in favor of the truth instead of falling in with the general trend toward denial. Perhaps he wants to please his colleagues, or his own parents, or himself. To do so, he betrays the little child he once was by professing this blatant untruth in front of millions of viewers. Unfortunately, his expert status will mean that he is taken seriously. This is one of the many forms in which people pass on the deception they have experienced to others, indeed to a huge audience, without accepting the responsibility for their actions or the reasons behind those actions.

13

We Can Identify
the Causes of Our
Sufferings

E MOTIONS REPRESSED IN childhood remain stored away in our bodies, and in adulthood they can cause symptoms of varying severity. We may suffer from bouts of depression, attacks of panic fear, or violent reactions toward our children without identifying the true causes of our despair, our fear, or our rage. If we were aware of those causes, it would prevent us from falling ill, because then we would realize that our fathers and mothers no longer have any power over us and can no longer subject us to physical "correction."

In most cases, however, we know nothing about the causes of our sufferings because the memories of those childhood beatings have long been consigned to total oblivion. Initially, this amnesia may be beneficial, acting as a protection for the child's brain. In the long term, however, it is disastrous because it then becomes chronic and has a profoundly confusing impact. Though it protects us from unpleasant memories, it cannot preserve us from severe symptoms like the unexplained fear constantly warning us of dangers that no 'longer exist. In childhood such fear would have been entirely realistic, for instance, in the case of a six-month-old girl whose mother regularly slapped her in order to "teach her obedience." Of course, the girl survived those slaps, and all the other physical punishments inflicted on her in youth. But at the age of forty-six she suddenly developed heart problems.

For years on end we trust to medication to alleviate our sufferings. But there is one question no one (neither patients nor their doctors) ever asks: *Where* is this danger that my body incessantly warns me of? The danger is hidden away in childhood. But all the doors that might afford us the right perspective on the problem appear to be hermetically closed. No one attempts to open them. On the contrary—we do everything we can to avoid facing up to our personal history and the intolerable apprehension that dogged us for so long in childhood. Such a perspective would reestablish contact with the most vulnerable and powerless years of our lives, and that is the last thing we want to think about. We have no desire to go through that feeling of desperate impotence all over again. On no account do we want to be reminded of the atmosphere that surrounded us when we were small and were helplessly exposed to the whims and excesses of power-hungry adults.

But this period is one that has an incomparably powerful impact on the rest of our lives, and it is precisely by confronting it that we can find the key to understanding our attacks of (apparently) groundless panic, our high blood pressure, our stomach ulcers, our sleepless nights, and—tragically—the seemingly inexplicable rage aroused in us by a small baby crying. The logic behind this enigma resolves itself once we set out to achieve awareness about the early stages of our lives. Seeking that awareness is the first step toward understanding our sufferings. And when we have taken that step, the symptoms that have plagued us for so long will gradually begin to recede. Our body no longer has any need of them, because now we have assumed conscious responsibility for the suffering children we once were.

Truly attempting to understand the child within means acknowledging and recognizing its sufferings rather than denying them. Then we can provide supportive company for that mistreated infant, an infant left entirely alone with its fears, deprived of the consolation and support that a "helping witness" could have provided. By offering guidance to the children we once were, we can create a new atmosphere they can respond to, helping them to see that it is not the whole world that is full of dangers, but above all the world of the family that they were doomed to fear in every moment of their existence. We never knew what bad mood might prompt our mother to expose us to the full force of her aggression. We never knew what we could do to defend ourselves. No one came to our aid, no one saw that we were in danger. And in the end we learned not to perceive that danger ourselves.

Many people manage to protect themselves from the memories of a nightmare childhood by taking medication of some kind, frequently of an antidepressive nature. But such medication only robs us of our true emotions, and then we are unable to find expression for the logical response to the cruelties we were exposed to as children. And this inability is precisely what triggered the illness in the first place.

Once we have chosen to embark on a course of therapy, all this should change. Now we have a witness for our sufferings, someone who wants to know what happened to us, who can help us learn how to free ourselves of the fear of being humiliated, beaten, and maltreated as we were before, a witness who can assist us in leaving the chaotic mess of our childhood behind, in identifying our emotions and ultimately living with the truth. Thanks to the sustaining presence of this person, we can abandon our denial and regain our emotional honesty.

What kind of people go in search of therapy? And why do they do so? In most cases they are women who feel that they have failed their children and who suffer from depression without recognizing it as such. Men usually come on the insistence of their partners, or because they are afraid of being abandoned, or because they are already separated.

Usually, the majority of these people totally idealize their childhood and find the punishments inflicted on them completely justified. They will frequently give impassive accounts of the cruelties they have suffered.

Therapies are normally expected to solve all our present problems and restore our well-being—but without forcing us to confront our more profound emotions. We fear those emotions as if they were our worst enemy. The pharmaceutical industry caters to these fears or buried emotions with a whole range of so-called remedies—Viagra for impotence, Xanax for anxiety, antidepressives to fend off the deleterious effects of depression. But there is no attempt to understand the deep-seated causes underlying these conditions.

Many therapists offer behavioral therapies to remedy the symptoms displayed by their patients rather than examining their significance and their causes. Their justification for so doing is that those causes cannot be identified. But this is simply not true. In every single case it is possible to identify the causes for the symptoms.

They are invariably hidden away in childhood. But only very few people truly want to confront their own histories.

Those exceptional individuals can do so by accepting their emotions for what they are. This is a course of action that we will only recoil from as long as we do not understand the causes of those emotions. Once therapy has enabled us to experience and understand the rage and fear inspired in us by our parents, we will no longer feel the compulsion to take out our anger on surrogate victims, usually our own children. In this way we can discover the reality of our own early biographies step by step, understand the sufferings of the children we once were, and become fully aware of the cruelty we were exposed to in our total isolation. Then we will realize that there were very good reasons for our anger and despair, because we were never understood, accepted, and taken seriously. By experiencing these unexpressed emotions we can learn to know ourselves better.

Many therapists themselves still live in a state of total denial and have never for one moment felt the sufferings of the children they once were. We can see this from their publications. They accuse me of transposing the things I went through in childhood onto all other cases, and they insist that my situation was exceptional. Unfortunately, this is not so, as I have experienced almost daily for decades. While reflection on this fact is still rare, there is a thinking minority of therapists who do their best to uncover their own repressed histories. After reading the articles on my Web site, they frequently ask questions that I shall attempt to answer here.

1. *Once we have realized how much suffering our parents inflicted on us, is there not a danger that we will hate them and perhaps no longer wish to see them?*

In my view this "risk" is negligible, because justified hatred that has been experienced and understood as such will resolve itself and leave us receptive for other emotions (see chapter 4, "What is Hatred?")—unless, that is, we force ourselves to prolong relationships that we do not want. If we do that, we put ourselves in a position of dependency that involves a repetition of the helplessness of the maltreated child. And this helplessness is the source of hatred. True, many people fear that they will lose the love they feel for their parents once they face up to the cruelty inflicted on them in childhood. But I see this as an advantage, not as a loss. The soul of the child needs the love from its parents in order to survive; it also needs the illusion of being loved in order not to have to face up to the fact that it is growing up in an emotional desert. But as adults we can live with the truth, and our bodies will be grateful to us for doing so. In some cases it is indeed not only possible but absolutely necessary to lose this "love," in fact to actively desist from sustaining it. It is only by way of self-delusion that individuals who have finally understood the children they once were can love the people who were cruel to them. Many people believe that their love for their parents is stronger than they are. But once we have reached adulthood, this is definitely not true. The idea that we are helplessly entrapped in that love derives from a child's view of things. Adults are free to invest their love in relationships where they can live out and express their true feelings without being made to suffer for it.

2. *Will understanding the reasons underlying our parents' cruelty help us to progress?*

I believe that the exact opposite is the case. As children, we all tried to understand our parents, and we do this all our lives.

Unfortunately, it is precisely this compassion for our parents that frequently prevents us from perceiving our own sufferings.

3. *Is it not selfish to think of ourselves before thinking of others? Is it not immoral to care more about ourselves than about others?*

No. A child's compassion will not alleviate the mother's depression as long as the mother denies the sufferings of her own childhood. There are mothers with very loving and caring adult children who still suffer from severe depression because they do not know that the reasons for their sufferings are to be found in their own childhood. The love they receive from their children can do nothing to change this. On the other hand, a child's persistent involvement with its parents can ruin his or her whole life. The prerequisite for true compassion for others is empathy with one's own destiny, something a maltreated child can never develop. On the contrary, such a child cannot allow itself to feel its own pain. A child forced to suppress its own emotions will have no compassion for itself and consequently no compassion for others. This encourages criminal behavior that is frequently concealed behind moral, religious, or apparently progressive political verbiage.

4. *Would it not be ideal for us to love both our old, enfeebled parents and the children we once were?*

If someone attacks us on the street, we are hardly likely to give him a hug and thank him for the blows he has dealt us. But children almost always do precisely that when their parents are cruel to them, because they cannot live without the illusion of being loved by them. They believe that everything the parents do to them is inspired by love. In therapy the adult client has to learn to forsake this infant position and live with reality. As

I have said, once you have learned to love yourself, you cannot love your tormentors at the same time.

Access to the history of our childhood gives us the freedom to be true to our own selves, which means feeling and recognizing our emotions and acting in accordance with our needs. This guarantees us good health and honest and genuine relationships with our relatives. We stop belittling and neglecting our bodies and our souls, and we also stop maltreating them in the same impatient, angry, and humiliating way as our parents once treated the little child that could not speak or make sense of what was going on. We can then attempt to understand the reasons for our distress, and this is easier once we have achieved awareness of our own history. No medication can tell us anything about the *causes* of our distress or our illnesses. Medication can only camouflage those reasons and alleviate the pain—for a while. But unrecognized causes still remain active. They continue to emit their signals until the outbreak of the next illness. That illness will then be treated with different medication, and that medication will again take no account of the causes for the disorder. But those causes are identifiable. All the sick person needs to do is to take an interest in the situation of the child he or she once was and actually experience the feelings clamoring for expression and comprehension.

14

How to Find
the Right Therapist

I AM FREQUENTLY asked what I consider to be the decisive
factor in successful psychotherapy. Is it realization of the truth
and the liberation from the injunction to keep silent and idealize one's parents, or is it the presence of an "enlightened witness"? I
believe that this is not a case of either-or, since both are essential.
Without an "enlightened witness," it is simply impossible to bear
the truth of early childhood. But for me an "enlightened witness" is
not just someone who has studied psychology or been through primal experiences with a guru. In my view, "enlightened witnesses"
are people who have found the courage to face up to their own
histories, thus achieving autonomy without having to compensate
for their repressed impotence by exercising power over others.

Adults need help in coping with present situations and at the
same time remaining in close contact with the knowing and suffering children they once were, children they have not dared to

listen to for so long but can now pay heed to in the company of an empathic witness. The body remembers everything done to it but cannot express itself in words. It is like the child we once were, the child that sees everything but remains helpless without the assistance of adults. So when emotions from the past rise to the surface, they are always accompanied by the fear of the vulnerable child that needs understanding, or at least reassurance, from adults. Puzzled parents unable to understand their children, because they are unaware of their own histories, can still provide this reassurance. They can alleviate their children's (and their own) fears by supplying protection, security, and continuity. In dialogue with our bodies, the cognitive system can do the same.

Unlike the body, the adult cognitive system knows little about events of long ago. Conscious memories are fragmentary and unreliable. But the cognitive system has extensive knowledge, a well-developed intellect, and a trove of experience that children cannot have. As adults are no longer helpless, they can give the inner child (the body) protection by listening to it, by enabling it to tell its stories in whatever way it can. In the light of these stories, the adult's mysterious and incomprehensible fears and emotions will begin to make sense. At last they are situated in a context and are no longer so menacing. In the company of someone ready to take the distress of children seriously, one is no longer alone with one's stories. This is where the therapist comes in.

I know how difficult it is to find the right therapist, but I believe it is possible if you know what you need and want. So here I shall try to answer some questions that may encourage you to test the candidate's attitude. (I have elected to refer to the therapist as "she," but of course both genders are meant).

What do I need to overcome my plight?

You need an honest, empathic person who can help you to take the knowledge stored in your body seriously, a person who has already successfully done that herself because she had the good fortune to find the kind of help you are looking for.

How can I find out if a therapist is that kind of person?

By asking a lot of questions.

This idea scares me. Why am I afraid of asking questions?

As a child, you were probably punished for asking questions because they might have shaken your parents' position of power. Perhaps your questions were ignored, or you were offered lies instead of truthful answers. This was very distressing. Now you fear that this might happen again. It may indeed be that you will not be understood or your questions will trigger the fears and defenses of the therapist. But remember that you are no longer a little child without any options. You can leave and look for another therapist. You can recognize lies, confusing responses, and defense strategies for what they are. You must take what you hear seriously. If you feel uneasy, do not deny this feeling, and never believe that you will be able to change the therapist's (the parents') attitude in future. You will not. She will need therapy herself, and this is not your job as long as you are paying her fee.

My suspicions make me feel guilty. If I cannot be trustful I shall never find out what is good for me.

Your suspicions have a history, as does your need for *special* understanding. Your parents and caregivers abused your trust. As a child, you felt this strongly because your body knew the truth. You could not develop any trust. Take what your body tells you seriously. What you are feeling is the mute, misunderstood child beginning to find its voice and clamoring for your affection. If you feel uneasy with a person, trust your feelings, do not shove them aside; try to find out what is disturbing you. If you feel truly understood by someone, your body will alert you to the fact immediately and very clearly by relaxing without having to undergo any special exercises. Perhaps the therapist will encourage you to ask questions. That in itself is a good sign, but pay close attention to her answers.

What do I risk by asking questions from the outset?

Nothing. You only stand to gain. If the answer is hostile, conspicuously incomplete, or defensive, you can save a lot of time and money by leaving on the spot. If, on the other hand, the response you receive is satisfactory, you will feel encouraged to ask further questions. And you should do precisely that. You can write down the questions you find particularly important and take them to the next interview.

What am I allowed to ask?

Whatever you need to know. Never forget to ask the therapist about her childhood and her experiences during her training. What is her opinion of her training and her teachers, what helped her, what did not? Is she open-minded enough to see what was wrong, or does she try to protect the people who harmed her? Does she play down this harm, perhaps asserting that she never was harmed? Was she beaten or otherwise humiliated as a child? What importance does she attach to this experience? Is she truly aware of the consequences of this experience for her later life, or does she deny its importance? Does she avoid confrontation with her own pain? Does she appreciate the immense significance of childhood, or does she deny it and still carry on behaving like a good child? If this is the case, she will attempt to deflect you from your purpose. Understandably, this will not always be easy for you to identify because you feel dependent on her.

Is it a good sign if she tells me she has read Alice Miller's Drama of the Gifted Child?

In itself it means nothing. Ask her what she felt when she read *For Your Own Good* and the other books, and ask her what criticisms she has of them. What helped her personally, what did not? A good therapist must help you to perceive and satisfy your own long-neglected needs, your need for freedom of speech, of understanding and being understood, your need to be respected and taken seriously, your need for frank, communicative exchanges with others. If you embark on that course and protect the child within, rage and hatred will gradually dwindle and probably, at some point, stop tormenting you altogether. Rage and hatred are alarm signals warning you that you are in the process of repeating your parents' neglect and their belittlement of you. As soon as you find a therapist able to help you recognize your real needs and comply with them, you will no longer need your parents for this task, and your rage can die away, though perhaps only until something else touches on the past stored in your body. But these periods will gradually become shorter, once the body has been allowed to mobilize its own regulation system. If we can recognize our most profound needs and also fulfill them, then we do not have to "immerse ourselves" in the feelings of the helpless child all our lives, as some primal therapists believe and recommend. But for this we require the right kind of assistance.

Is it not impertinent to ask so many questions?

Not at all. It is your right to ask for the information you require, and the therapist must have the courage, self-confidence, and sincerity to give you the appropriate answers. Otherwise she is not the right therapist for you.

Am I not looking for an ideal that does not exist?

I don't think so. In some forums you will see that sincerity, attentiveness, compassion, courage, and openness *do* exist. Why should you not expect these characteristics from your therapist?

I fully realize that you may not be able to follow all this advice if you are in a state of distress. But perhaps it will stiffen your resolve, especially over and against therapists who play the great discoverer but who get annoyed, offended, or even aggressive when someone questions them. If you were treated this way when you were a child, you may be quickly discouraged and intimidated. If that happens, ask for another explanatory interview. Good luck!

15

Answers to Readers' Letters

Introduction to Letters Section

I am occasionally asked how I can be so sure of myself in contra-
dicting established opinions. After all, I do not belong to any school
of thought, any cult or other community of the like-minded that
supplies so many people with what they believe to be the "right"
answers. So what is my confidence based on? It is indeed true that
I only believe in facts I can test for myself. My access to these facts
is based on my own experience and on the thousands of letters I
have received from the readers of my books since the appearance
of *The Drama of the Gifted Child* in 1979. I have frequently felt
the desire to respond to these letters and greatly regretted that for
reasons of time I have not been able to do so. Another desire I felt
was to make these important testimonies and accounts by victims
of childhood cruelty available to others. But this I could not do
because it would have been a breach of confidence.

Only in 2005 did I hit upon the idea of establishing a mailbox on my Web site, where letters of general interest could be published with the consent of their authors. This provided the writers of these letters with a platform where they could express themselves freely and seek ways of liberating themselves from the tragic consequences of childhood abuse in the company of others. In this book I shall be publishing only a small number of my answers. The readers' letters themselves can be found under "Readers' Mail" on the Web site, complete with title and date.

The striking thing about most of these letters is the way they reflect an almost total denial of reality by the people who have written them. They tell of unimaginable torments that the writers have never acknowledged as such despite years of therapy. The letters are almost always written from the perspective of the parents, parents who were totally unable to tolerate, let alone love, their children. The children's perspective finds no expression whatsoever, except in the sufferings of the adults they have become, the physical symptoms, the bouts of depression, the thoughts of suicide, the crippling feelings of guilt. The writers of these letters constantly insist that they were never abused as children, that the only physical "correction" they received was an occasional slap of no consequence at all, or a kick or two they had richly deserved because they sometimes behaved abominably and got on their parents' nerves. I am frequently assured that deep down these people were loved by their fathers and mothers, and if they were cruelly treated from time to time, it was because things just got too much for their parents, who were unhappy, depressed, uninformed, or possibly even alcoholics, and all because they themselves had been deprived of love when they were young. So it is hardly surprising that these parents were quick to lose their tempers and take their unhappiness and resentment out on their children. Such behavior is, after all, readily understandable, is it not? The dearest wish of these children was to help their parents, because they loved them and felt sorry for them. But however hard they tried, they never managed to free them from their depression and make them happy.

The tormenting feelings of guilt triggered by this failure are unrelenting and implacable. What have I done wrong, these people ask themselves, why have I failed to free my parents from their misery? I try the best I can. My therapists tell me to enjoy the good things in life, but I can't, and that makes me feel guilty too. They tell me to grow up, to stop seeing myself as a victim; my childhood is a thing of the past, I should turn over a new leaf and stop agonizing. They tell me not to put the blame on others, otherwise my hatred will kill me. I should forgive and forget and live in the present, otherwise I'll turn into a "borderline patient," whatever that is. But how can I do that? Of course, I don't want to put the blame on my parents, I love them, and I owe my life to them. They had trouble enough with me. But how can I banish my guilt feelings? They get even more overpowering when I hit my children. It's awful, but I can't stop doing it, it's driving me to despair. I hate myself for this compulsive violence, I disgust myself when I fly into an uncontrollable rage. What can I do to stop it? Why must I hate myself all the time and feel guilty? Why were all those therapists unable to help me? For years I've been trying to follow their advice, but I still can't manage to dispel my feelings of guilt and love myself as I should.

Let me quote my answer to one letter that contained all these elements:

"In your first letter you said you had never been cruelly treated as a child. In this one you tell me that when you were young, you were cruel to your dog because you were a naughty child. Who taught you to see things that way? The point is that no single child anywhere on earth will be cruel to his or her dog without having been severely maltreated. But there are a whole lot of people who see themselves as you do and whose guilt feelings drive them to despair. Their sole concern is not to see their parents' guilt because they fear the punishment they would incur for putting the blame where it belongs. If my books have not helped you to understand this, there is nothing more I can do for you. You can only help yourself by no longer protecting your parents from your own justified feelings. Then you will be free of the compulsive urge to imitate them by hating yourself, blaming yourself, and describing yourself as a monster."

How can someone love themselves if the message that they were not worth loving was drummed into them at an early stage? If they were beaten black and blue to make them into a different person? If they had it impressed on them that they were a nuisance to their parents, and that nothing in the world would ever change their parents' dislike and anger? They will believe that they are the cause of this hatred, though that is simply not true. They feel guilty, they try to become a better person, but this can never succeed because the parents take out on their own children the rage they had to suppress and hold back in their dealings with their own parents. The child was merely the butt of this rage.

Once we have realized this, thanks to the body language implicit in physical symptoms, we stop waiting for the love of our parents, and we know why it will never materialize. Only then can we allow ourselves to see how we were treated as children and to feel how we suffered as a result. Instead of understanding and commiserating with our parents, instead of blaming ourselves, we start taking sides with the abused child we once were. This is the moment when we start loving that child, but this love can never come about without the prior insight into the tragedy we were involved in as youngsters. This is when we stop playing down our sufferings and embark on a respectful engagement with them *and* with the child. The doors barring us off from our own selves suddenly swing open. But we can never open those doors just by telling someone "You should love yourself." A person receiving such advice will be completely confounded by it as long as he or she is cut off from the knowledge of what their childhood was really like and why the truth is so painful.

My conviction is that therapy is only successful if it can change this perspective and the thought patterns connected with it. If people genuinely succeed in feeling how they suffered from their parents' behavior as children, they will usually lose their empathy for those parents with hardly any inner conflict at all. They will train their affections on the children they once were. But for this change of perspective to succeed, we need a witness who sides fully with the child and does not hesitate to condemn the deeds of that child's parents. Genuine "enlightened witnesses" can help us to abandon denial and face up to our own past, so that we can finally leave it behind without feelings of guilt. Knowledge of our histories and our feelings enables us to find out who we are and to give ourselves what we so badly need but never received from our parents: love and respect.

The following is my response, dated 28 August 2006, to a reader who asked me what I meant by "uncovering therapy," a form of therapy that has proved effective both for myself and others.

I call therapy "uncovering" if it helps clients to get to know their own suppressed, painful childhood history with the help of reawakened feelings and dreams. Then they need no longer fear the dangers that threatened them in childhood but now threaten them no more. These clients stop unconsciously fearing and repeating what happened to them at such a tender age because they know their childhood reality and can respond to it with rage and grief in the company of a therapist acting as an empathic witness. They stop treating themselves like nobodies, blaming themselves, harming themselves with all kinds of addictions, because they have now been able to develop empathy for the child that suffered so severely from the parents' behavior. If in their adult lives they should be threatened by dangers, they will be better equipped to withstand them because they understand their old fears and can assess them for what they were.

This kind of procedure differs crucially from the kinds of treatment that involve practicing new behavior or improving one's well-being (via yoga, meditation, positive thinking, or whatever). Here the subject of childhood is invariably skirted. Fear of it is ubiquitous in our society. I trace it to the fear felt by abused children, the fear of the next blow that is bound to follow if they should dare to see through their parents' cruelty.

Psychoanalytic theory is also grounded in this fear of the parents. Sometimes for decades on end, clients and analysts remain bogged down in a maze of half-baked concepts, permanently suffering from guilt feelings because they made it so difficult for their parents to understand their "disturbed" children. In all this they frequently have no idea that they were in fact severely abused children. Whether therapists will be able to make this knowledge accessible will depend on what they know about their own lives and their first few years. To clear up these questions I have compiled a FAQ [frequently asked questions] list [see chapter 14, "How to

Find the Right Therapist,"] that can give people guidance on what they need to know before they enter into an attachment.

Of course, these people still face many questions they have evaded so far. My answers, which follow in this section, are attempts to help them get their bearings in this new situation and find therapists who will stand by them as empathic and "enlightened" witnesses and make full use of the knowledge thus gained.

Should I Confront My Family with the Truth?

Sometimes confrontation with the parents is necessary in order to get a grip on the truth if one has a tendency to deny that truth to oneself. But if it has been clearly identified in all its grimness, then direct confrontation is not absolutely necessary. The strong desire for confrontation may be conditioned by the hope that we may have been wrong in our judgment, or that the parents may have changed in the meantime. In other words, we may be hoping that they will understand us after all if we only manage to explain things to them properly.

Sometimes we believe that we will feel stronger in the face of our old, enfeebled parents. This may be the case, but I wouldn't bank on it. The small child's latent fear, still effective in the adult, is very strong and may accompany us all our lives. The task of therapy is to enable us to experience it consciously, understand its justification and thus overcome it. If therapy succeeds in doing this, there is usually little need for confrontation with the parents. Sometimes conflicts with our siblings can be avoided in this way, especially if we are able to accept and respect their fears because we know from experience how persistent those fears can be.

We can only overcome our *own* fear, jettison our *own* denial. We cannot do this for our brothers and sisters. If they prefer not to embark on this path, then we are powerless to intervene. It is distressing for us not to have "enlightened witnesses" in our siblings, but we must learn to accept this as our fate. In the course of time we may find friends who have been through similar experiences, and they may become "enlightened witnesses."

Some people find a way of overcoming the fear of their overweening, menacing parents by writing letters to them that they never send. Here they can give an uncensored voice to the small child they once were and in the course of writing admit, and actually feel, for the first time, the bitter disappointment, helpless rage, crushing indignation, and ultimately the endless grief that have been condemned to silence for decades. Confrontation with the actual parents is no substitute.

I wish you every success for your therapy.

(*7 July 2005*)

Fear of the Truth

I have obviously failed to arouse your indignation and encourage you to rebel. You still write like a good girl practicing philosophical forbearance. You describe the facts very clearly, but you obviously feel nothing. Emotionally, you are still waiting for your parents' love. You try to understand them, to suppress feelings like rage and indignation, and you are living in a small child's panic fear of your parents' brutality. But you are also asking questions. Perhaps this letter is the beginning of the long-overdue rebellion your body has been waiting for to finally rid itself of those superfluous pounds with the help of justified, healthy rage. You tell me clearly how your tolerance for your parents and the complete absence of rebellion and anger are destroying your life and forcing you to carry the weight of your parents' crimes in your own body. Those 260 pounds are hardly anything other than the burden of the abuse inflicted on a tender, bright, and intelligent girl.

P.S.: Today's letter telling me that your body sweated for an hour when you attempted to imagine your father as a monster confirms my conjecture.

(21 July 2005)

What Is Therapy?

It is never too late to ask your therapist. Her answers will show how close she herself has got to the goal you have set yourself. To find out the truth about one's own childhood at all costs, as you are trying to do, one needs the kind of assistance that makes that possible, certainly not someone who makes you feel unsure of yourself. A therapist still living in infant fear of her internalized parents and denying her traumas will hardly be able to provide this kind of assistance. Professional training of the conventional kind will not protect anyone from sustaining such a defensive attitude.

On my Web site you will find suggestions for questions that can help you to determine whether your therapist has achieved the inner freedom and authenticity she needs to have for you to go in search of your own truth with her assistance. My recent articles on the Web site (see, e.g., "The Longest Journey") also offer advice in finding the right therapist. Inspired by some of the last letters addressed to me, I shall attempt to outline here what I understand by successful therapy. I should, however, emphasize that my ideas on this point are not in line with the prevailing trends. They will only be helpful for people truly desirous of getting to know the children they once were and determined to pursue that goal to the end.

In my eyes, the conditions that must be fulfilled if therapy is to be successful are the following:

1. The therapist must side unequivocally with the injured child. She will display indignation at the things done to the child and will not hide her feelings behind a show of neutrality. This will enable the client to gain access to his or her feelings. In the process, childhood reality will reveal itself with increasing clarity.

2. Present problems causing strong emotions can also be drawn upon to uncover childhood reality. Insight into that world will help to understand the present emotions (triggers).

3. Constant interaction between the past and the present generates knowledge about the client's own story and identity. This knowledge imparts a sense of security previously unknown.

4. Once the client has achieved the ability to cope with old feelings and to make productive use of the "triggers," there is no further need of the therapist's presence.

(24 July 2005)

The Role of Flashbacks

Your letter is clear proof of the way in which the ignorance of some doctors and parents continues to keep the causes of an "illness" (basically a disorder of functional logic) in the dark. What you tell me about instruction at school is also revealing. The phenomenon you describe is not uncommon. The threatened child protects itself by dissociating itself from its perceptions, experiencing itself as it were from outside its own body, from the ceiling of the room where the abuse happened. Former victims of sexual abuse frequently say that they experience themselves in this way. They were thus able to keep the truth and the pain at bay until the memories broke through and their symptoms disappeared. It is highly unfortunate that the attempt is made to cover over such salutary and—as your example shows—such liberating processes with medication or theories, and that so many so-called experts connive in this attempt.

(8 September 2005)

Why Are Children Badly Treated?

Children are badly treated because their parents were badly treated as well, though they deny the fact emotionally, in the same way that you do. If this were not the case, you would not ask this question, particularly as, at least intellectually, you already know the answer. I wish you courage and perspicacity in your further life!

(10 September 2005)

You Are Not Malicious

There is no way of avoiding rage when you start to understand, to feel, and to open your eyes. Your anger is strong, powerful, and very definitely justified. It will lead to rebellion and liberation. But do not overtax yourself with your primal therapy! Take things step-by-step, assisted by a therapist who is neither afraid of your history nor her own. Do not rush any fences! You are not alone. You feel deserted because the emotions from your childhood are telling you how lonely you were. This child was alone and forced to keep silent. But now, as an adult, you are speaking out. You are writing, and you touch others in the process. You are no longer alone, as you were before, even if you feel that you are. And you are not malicious! Your anger is more than justified, and now you finally—and fortunately!—know that.

(21 September 2005)

You Cannot Force Anyone to Open Their Hearts

You quote your former partner as saying: "I don't want any more of this relationship, I can't stand the pressure." I'm afraid you have no choice but to respect this decision and desist from putting pressure on your friend, particularly as you tell me how truly fond of him you are.

If I were you, I would, however, ask myself why I should have to love a person who rejects me, who finds my love a nuisance and drives me into such a state of distraction. Why do I love someone who makes me suffer so much, who is not honest with me, so that I cannot understand him? How does this tie in with my childhood? You have probably already asked yourself these questions, otherwise you would not have written to me rather than someone else. After all, you know of my interest in the consequences of a traumatic childhood.

I believe that we can only truly understand ourselves. We may be able to understand others if they want us to and let us into their feelings. But if they refuse that point blank and close themselves off entirely, unwilling to tell us the reasons for such sudden rejection, then all attempts to understand are futile—unless we actively enjoy trying to crawl up the walls.

(2 October 2005)

The Fourth Commandment

I consider your letter a well meant but misguided attempt to reconcile two absolutely opposing views (mine and that of the Bible) by means of interpretations. One of the things this Web site and the letters published here demonstrate is the immense amount of suffering the Fourth Commandment has actually caused in parenting and upbringing. For me, only the facts count, not interpretations or theories. For thousands of years interpretations and theories have helped to camouflage the truth about the perverted cruelties inflicted on children in the name of upbringing and religion. Such children are bound to fall ill in the aftermath. Accordingly, I have never had any part in such speculations.

(3 October 2005)

So Much Courage in Spite of All

I am grateful to you for your frank and wise letter. It is rare and astounding that a woman so cruelly mistreated and rejected by her parents should find the strength and determination to go in search of herself as you have—and with such tenacity. You can see from the reactions of your body that you cannot only withstand your own truth (infinitely painful as it is), you can also profit from these insights. Your letter will help others to summon up the courage to face their grief and disillusionment, rather than punishing themselves all their lives for the deeds committed by their parents.

(4 October 2005)

Are Women Less Aggressive than Men?

In my view women are by no means less aggressive than men. Of course, they are victimized and disadvantaged by men avenging themselves for the beatings they received from their mothers. But women avenge themselves for such victimization and physical cruelty by taking it out on their little children, thus breeding new generations of avengers who consciously love and honor their parents.

I see no real difference between the cruelty of women and that of men, because both sexes have learned such sadism at the hands of their parents and caregivers at a time when their brains were still in the process of formation. As children, they were subjected to cruelty and even perversion, but they were not allowed to defend themselves. So later they take out their repressed anger on other defenseless people, frequently in the same way their parents treated them when they were small. Women frequently vent this acquired sadism on their children, while men also give free rein to it by victimizing employees at work or lower military ranks, or else participating in orgies of violence like genocide or terrorist attacks. The causes invariably lie in the repressed and totally denied sufferings of their childhood (though most of them will insist that they had wonderful parents). People who were not humiliated, tormented, or beaten in their early years are incapable of sadism.

Women can live out all kinds of covert perversion on their children and torment them with impunity as long as they call this behavior "good parenting." Society idealizes mothers because people have never consciously realized that their own mothers treated them cruelly when they were small. Accordingly, women normally enjoy total immunity.

I see no sex-specific differences in the suicide bombers. I understand terrorism as an attempt to compensate for the humiliations these people were subjected to, but have never consciously perceived as such, by means of a "magnificent deed" (such as sacrificing their own lives for the sake of a group).

Though it is not difficult to understand this dynamic, there are not many people who would allow themselves to give up their denial and look the truth in the face. The fear felt by the tormented children they once were can prevent this all their lives.

(8 October 2005)

Violence against Babies

I fully understand your indignation and horror at the violence perpetrated on babies. Similar feelings prompted me to do my research, write my books, and establish my Web site. To my astonishment, I quickly realized that very few people take an interest in this taboo subject. Nowhere did I find people who were prepared to listen to me. Recently, I intended to write an article about a mother who had killed all nine of her babies, but no newspaper was interested in publishing it. And when I took the case of Jessica as an example of how infanticide can come about, the journalists I approached behaved like apprehensive churchmen. Nor have I ever been able to persuade the Vatican to express compassion for maltreated babies. Everywhere I have encountered total indifference.

In 1980, I referred in my book *For Your Own Good* to nineteenth-century upbringing manuals that instructed parents to instill "good manners" into their children from the outset by means of "physical correction." I expected this to open people's eyes, but no response was forthcoming. In France I commissioned a statistical survey to find out what percentage of mothers struck their children and how old these children were when they were first given a beating. Again the response was almost nil.

All these experiences have taught me that what you call normal behavior toward a baby—the desire to protect it—is unfortunately the exception. Obviously, the "normal" thing is to bring up little children with slaps and smacks and to inflict pain and fear on them. Why? Because the people who do this kind of thing received the same treatment when they were young and at the same time had the grotesque information drummed into them that it was all for their own good. Repressed rage vents itself later on these people's own children. You are quite right. The smaller the child, the more omnipotent the adult feels, and the more profoundly he or she hopes that the memories of early cruelty stored in the body can be obliterated in this way.

A major enlightenment campaign for the entire population is urgently necessary. Perhaps you have an idea about how this could be organized. Unfortunately, hardly anyone is interested in starting such a campaign because almost all of us were beaten in infancy and were forced to learn that this treatment was good for us. Most people adhere to this belief all their lives and bring up their children in the same way they themselves were brought up. In this way they can protect themselves from the realization that they were abused when they were small. On no account do they want to know that with every blow they inflict on their children they are abusing them and damaging them for life, be it "only" by destroying their capacity for empathy and logical thinking.

(22 October 2005)

Repressed Rage

Your depression is telling you that you are repressing your strongest feelings. If you take antidepressants you will also be repressing the truth, your own personal truth. You love your parents, and in the night you are assailed by bouts of rage. Luckily, you can still feel it! I hope your therapist can help you understand who deserves your anger and why. If the child subjected to cruelty feels the presence of a courageous witness, then you will no longer need medication. You will become sentient again and understand the causes of your sufferings.

(9 January 2006)

Forgiveness Manipulates Feelings

The question you raise is extremely important. But it rests on the naïve supposition that we can manipulate our feelings without making others pay the price. In reality, we cannot do that. You say what everyone else says, the things we all learned from our parents, in school, in church, and even from most therapists: "Turn over a new page!" It is all very well to be told to tell hatred that it should disappear and never rear its ugly head again. We all want to turn over a new page and live in peace. Everyone wants that, and it would be marvelous if it worked. But it doesn't. Why? Because, like all other emotions, rage will not let itself be dictated to or manipulated. Instead, it imposes its dictates on us, it forces us to feel it and to understand its causes. It can always return when we have been injured or affronted, and there is nothing we can do about it. Our bodies cannot turn over a new page; they insist that we listen to them.

Of course, we can try to repress our rage. The consequences are illness, addiction, and crime. If we do not want to feel our justified anger because we have already forgiven even our parents' worst depredations, we will soon realize to our surprise that we have been passing on to our children, or others, the same pain inflicted on us by our parents. If we are honest, we will not assert that we have acted "for their own good," or that cruelty is a valuable factor in parenting. Unfortunately, most parents do go around saying that, which is why our society is so mendacious.

(21 January 2006)

How Can We Live with This Knowledge?

Your question is one that I have been asked on various occasions, though perhaps never so trenchantly. My response has always been to inquire whether the person in question would prefer to retrace their steps, whether they would in fact be willing to live as before, without the knowledge they have gained. So far, no one has ever answered this question in the affirmative. Many say that they now have fewer "friends," but those they have are true friends, people who are also in search of themselves, who react less defensively, who feel no urge to proffer unwanted advice and can speak freely about their feelings. Communication thus becomes much easier. Most insist that they would never want to go back to the stage when they were separated from their own selves. Then they felt lonely even when they were surrounded by other people. Today they feel less lonely because they have a better understanding of themselves and their histories.

(25 January 2006)

Understanding Your Children's Feelings

I congratulate you on your success, even though your work is not yet over. But you have achieved the most important thing: you have established contact with yourself and your own history. Now nothing can go wrong. Your concern that you might not be able to "deal with" your child may be part of the history of your own childhood. Children who are not tormented have no need of tormenting others. When they are small, we have to pick them up when we are crossing the road, and later we can teach them a great deal without frightening them. But the more completely you see through the attitudes of your parents and caregivers, the more distinctly you will now sense how you suffered at their hands. You will learn to live in freedom and find it easier to understand your own feelings and those of your children. We only neglect, frighten, and maltreat our children as long as we deny that we were treated cruelly in childhood ourselves and forced to regard such cruelty as beneficial. In your case there appears to be no more danger of this happening.

(8 February 2006)

No University Chair on the Origins of Child Abuse

I believe it to be important to spread knowledge about the origins of child abuse in earlier generations. Although so many people have been victims of such abuse, there is still no university chair anywhere in the world devoted to the investigation of this phenomenon. For years I have been reading accounts of the cruelty inflicted on these people, and I know a great deal about the delayed consequences of such treatment. It is this that convinces me that enlightenment about the danger of hitting small children should be given major priority. The ignorance of the parents and the fear of adult children to clearly see the deeds of their parents committed in the name of upbringing and to call them by name *can* be done away with if we have the courage to talk about this subject in public.

(*11 February* 2006)

Illness Symptoms as the Language of the Body

Reading your account, I found myself reminded of Franz Kafka and his novella *The Metamorphosis*. We have here the case of a highly gifted, intelligent child whose mother has an appalling desire for control and an extreme tendency to violate boundaries, while the father categorically refuses to engage in any kind of communication. In these circumstances, how can the child come to terms with his or her fate without falling seriously ill? The symptoms of illness are the only genuine language left. You have elected to write down your story, and you have taken fifty pages to do so. But your body will continue to spur you on, to insist that you take your childhood sufferings seriously and listen to the child you once were.

Of course, you are right. What you definitely need is someone to stand by you. We cannot descend alone into the hell that you survived as a child. But where does one find such assistance? Your description of the mentality of today's therapists is probably very accurate; it might almost provide you with material for a play that would show the audience the roots of their own experiences. But that would not solve your problem. You need someone who will take an interest in your story because she knows her own and would like to work with you. You might shop around, testing therapists by asking them the questions I propose in my FAQ list, or giving them the story of your childhood to read and then deciding whether you are willing or able to entrust yourself to them. It may be that you are only too willing to tolerate ignorance because you were programmed to do so at such an early stage. But if you let yourself be guided by the responses to your story, then you will not run any risk. Try to understand the distress signals emitted by your body as a plea not to treat it the same way your mother treated you.

There are many people living lives like yours, but they cannot express themselves so well. They suffer from their attachment to their abusive parents, they feel guilty for what their parents did to them, and they squander their remaining energy in doing so.

I wish you luck in your search for a suitable therapist and the courage to ask your questions. You have to ask those questions! They will give you the necessary guidance. I only hope you find someone prepared to answer them. Until you have found someone, you might try spending your sleepless nights telling your mother how things are for you and filling her in on your present feelings for her—including what you wanted to tell her as a child but never dared to. You can also write to your father or an imaginary therapist without actually sending the letter. As soon as you address the person directly, your feelings will surface. Today no one will punish you for it. You will free yourself from the prison to which you have been consigned for so long and which has blocked off your path to the genuine, meaningful, and rich life you are entitled to.

(1 March 2006)

Breaking with Tradition

No, there is no reason to keep on running around in circles once we stop trying to understand parents who have no desire to understand themselves. Your mother worships your father who lashed her mercilessly with his belt. What is there to understand in that? And why should you want to? Because you grew up in that tradition? But there's nothing to stop you from breaking with it. At all events, it is time for you to try to understand yourself and to discover the feelings of the beaten child within.

(5 March 2006)

Forgiveness—Escape from Yourself

Your mother has told you that you were beaten at a very early age. You cannot remember either the mental or the physical pain of the little child forced to repress its sufferings. But multiple sclerosis is your body's way of reviving this pain when something in the present reminds you of it (for example, the feeling of not being understood by anyone when you are in a state of extreme distress). If your analyst is unwilling to even countenance this possibility, try to find a therapist who is not afraid of your story.

Your analyst's recommendations are in my view an instance of what makes us ill by suffocating justified rage. Reconciliation can provide relief for a while, because it mitigates the tormenting feelings of guilt. When we forgive the cruelty inflicted on us, we feel like a good—and hence beloved—child. But the body insists on the truth.

When I was a child, I did everything I could to understand my parents, and presumably like most analysts I continued "successfully" with those efforts for decades. But this was precisely what prevented me from discovering the child that had suffered torments at their hands. I did not know this child. Not in the slightest. I knew only the sufferings of my parents, I knew those of my patients and friends, but not my own. Only when I gave up trying to understand my parents' childhood (not least because they had no desire to do so themselves) was I able to feel the full extent of my pain and fear. Only then did I gradually discover the story of my childhood; only then did I begin to understand my fate. And that was when I lost the physical symptoms that had been trying in vain for so long to tell me my truth, while I listened to my patients and through their destinies began to achieve an inkling of what happens to beaten children. I realized that I had betrayed myself. Like many analysts, I had no idea who I really was, because I was fleeing from my own self and thought I could help others by doing so. Today, I believe that the best way of understanding others is to understand oneself.

(5 March 2006)

Children Must Believe in Their Mothers' Love

I can readily imagine that my letter shocked you, but I believed it permissible, indeed necessary, to inflict this shock on you so as to shake you out of your lethargy. Children always love their mothers, and they have to believe in their mothers' love in order not to die. Accordingly, they interpret even the worst cruelty as a sign of love. But if the adult you manages to engage in an exchange with your child inside, then he will have a lot to explain to him, and the child will understand that, quite definitely, though it may take some time for him to do so.

(6 March 2006)

How Can I Free Myself without Falling?

I can quite imagine that you have to vomit when you read my books because they indicate a course that you are terrified of embarking on, that of taking the mercilessly beaten little girl you once were into your arms and protecting her from her cruel parents. They tell you never to believe again that you have to love the people who injured that child so seriously (a child that you are now solely responsible for). This step frightens you, but the fear you feel is the consequence of the beatings and abuse you suffered. Who would not be afraid in the face of such a story? But you can do something to overcome that fear.

You cannot help your mother. Only she could do that, if she wanted to. And if you want to lead a meaningful life, you must stop betraying the child that suffered so much at her hands and the hands of a brutal father. This child has no one except you.

(*14 March 2006*)

Long Breast-Feeding

Your question is one I have frequently been asked. My answers have usually been misunderstood because everything I write is based on observation and not on ideology. The crucial point is that children always want to conform to their mothers' wishes. When they feel that their mother is lonely and is emotionally and sexually dependent on the continuation of breast-feeding, then they will behave, up to the age of seven years, in such a way that she believes they still need the breast. To my mind, to enjoy this response is a selfish abuse of the child's real need for autonomy. The upshot may be that the opportunities for developing self-awareness offered by life at the age of two, three, or four may be missed out on, thus cementing almost lifelong dependence on the mother. As always, what we need to ask here is the extent to which our behavior is dictated by our own childhood (mother) and to which we feel free to recognize the *true* needs of the child. In some tribes greatly admired and emulated by many women, children are breast-fed for a long time as a way of preventing another pregnancy. But as soon as a new child is born, the older child is weaned from one day to the next and left to its own devices, while the mother turns to the care of the newborn child with the same zeal. Was it the needs of the child that she was attempting to gratify for many years, or her own?

(16 March 2006)

Illusions of Love

You have definitely not killed off your feelings, otherwise your letter and your sufferings would not have moved me as they did. My impression is that your intellect is not an escape (as it is with so many people) but a source of strength. And if you allow yourself to make full use of that strength, you will manage to free yourself from your confusion by relinquishing your self-destructive love for your father and giving it to the little girl who was ignored, betrayed, and misled by both parents.

Perhaps you think you could never give up this love because it is stronger than you are. Many women believe this, if they are still somehow living in their own childhood and have never been allowed to grow up. But you are mistaken. As an adult, you are stronger than this love, and you can free yourself of it once you realize that you no longer need it. In childhood you were dependent on that love. Because you were forced to grow up with a brutal stepfather and a mendacious mother, your illusions of love for your biological father were indispensable for your inner self. But now they are destroying and confusing you. Why should you (have to) love a father who treated you like dirt, who inflicted so much suffering on you, who destroyed your self-respect? You owe him no love, only the anger that you are holding back in order to be a good girl and to be loved and finally accepted for what you are by someone who is obviously incapable of love. But this self-subjection is destroying your dignity and generating fear in the relationships you enter into. In those relationships you fear the effects of your love for your father. And you are right.

(*26 March 2006*)

Freeing the Child Within from Feelings of Guilt

Your letter is harrowing because it so clearly pronounces what others feel but never dare to express. At the end of it you ask, "What else can I do but to perceive and accept the lamenting and the tears of the child within as part of myself?" Perhaps my response will shock you, but I can only answer by saying what I think. It is not enough to perceive the tearful child as long as we still "love" the parents who caused its sufferings. Most people blame themselves for their parents' cruel behavior because they still feel attached to them. By doing so, they betray the tearful child and leave it in the custody of the parents for life instead of rescuing it from them.

You were never to blame for your parents' addictions and evasions. Never! And you are equally blameless now. Try to free yourself of the feelings of blame that have been foisted onto you. Children are not responsible for changing their parents. Only the parents can do that, if they wish to.

(*21 April 2006*)

Lost Childhood

You write: "This time I want to open myself to find out what happened to me psychologically in those nine years of darkness. I would dearly like to know, though I am fairly sure (no idea why) that it will be a great strain for me." Why do you have "no idea," although you recount very clearly what happened and give a detailed account of the misery, rejection, and total abandonment you experienced in your childhood? It comes apparent from what you say that you know a great deal but prefer not to believe it, not to see the *truth* of it because that would have killed you when you were small. You fear that pain as if you were still a child. But you are not. You know this, and you want to admit to the pain for the sake of your children, but also—fortunately—for the sake of the little girl you once were, the little girl no one showed any understanding for, the little girl who had to learn not to feel. Now you want to open up to your feelings, and I have no doubt that you will succeed. I hope you will manage to do what your mother should have done: to discover the richly endowed, intelligent, bright, life-affirming girl you were and love her for what she is. For a long time—much too long—you have treated yourself the way your mother treated you. No wonder you cannot stand her company. The rage that will hopefully materialize at some point is fully justified.

(26 April 2006)

No Longer in Danger

"None of this is easy," you write. I believe you, but I must add that this ordeal is right and proper and absolutely necessary. And you will succeed. You ask whether it is usual to have so many early memories. No, it is anything but usual; in my experience it is very rare. But it is quite normal for bad memories to be played down, which is something you do to excess. You are thirty-nine, and only a few days ago (!) you realized that your mother is not some perfect, supernatural being. Where have you been living? Was it your many dependencies that alienated you from reality? You know a great deal, but you do not allow yourself to draw conclusions from it. Why? You tell me yourself that you were thrashed from one end of the house to the other when you were small. What did you do with this knowledge to stop yourself from breaking out in a towering rage at the thought of it? You have grown up now. As you so rightly say, no one can beat you any longer. So what do you fear *today*?

If you let yourself feel the harm your parents have done to you with their exaggerated expectations and complete lack of understanding, leaving you alone at night, beating you black and blue, destroying your (conscious) feelings (which luckily live on in your body), then you will possibly give up your dependencies very quickly. They are the price you had to pay as a child in order not to see what your parents were really like and how destructive their treatment was. But now you are no longer a child, and you can afford to *take a very close look*, knowing that you are no longer in danger.

(27 April 2006)

What Now?

Your letter, your freedom to see, and your need to share your absolutely crucial knowledge have both gratified and surprised me, because such a clear-cut attitude is extremely rare. What normally paralyzes these abilities is the fear of the abused child in the face of the abusive parents and the strong attachment to them. In *The Truth Will Set You Free*, I attempt to explain the origins of this almost universal emotional blindness as the product of mental blockades in the first few years of life. But you appear to have escaped that fate and genuinely want to know how your childhood has marked you. How have you managed to preserve this healthy curiosity? Did you have influential "helping witnesses" who encouraged you to keep your eyes open for abuse?

You ask where you can find others with whom you can enter into an exchange on your insights. I do not know, but I have no doubt that you will find such people as soon as you have identified yourself and your own story. Then you will no longer let yourself be deceived by lies and fine-sounding bunkum. Perhaps the Internet can help you in your search.

(*9 May 2006*)

Where Is the Logic?

The logic is clear. It consists in sparing the parents, playing down their cruelties, denying our own true feelings and our knowledge. At all costs. What else must a father say beyond "I'll kill you one day!" for a daughter to consider herself mistreated?

(*18 May 2006*)

Fear of Fear

You cannot force memories to return, neither with meditation nor autogenic training. And everything that is forced is no good to you anyway. To get nearer the child you once were and empathize with her sufferings, you might try questioning your body when it draws attention to itself with symptoms. What does your "illness" consist in? Can you describe it? Can you say what emotions figure when the symptoms recur? Fear? Shame? Anger? Try to commit your dialogue with your body to paper, preferably lying down. And if you do decide in favor of therapy, read my FAQ list beforehand. If you are afraid of asking your potential therapist the questions you find there, do not attempt to suppress that fear, give in to it! It may tell you more about your early childhood than enforced metaphorical but unemotional memories or neurological examinations. You need not be afraid of your fear, it is always rooted in your childhood. But this can only be understood if we do not flee from this feeling but take it seriously. No one actively wants to feel how terrible it was to fear our young parents when we were tiny, to see them lose control, hear them ranting and raving, and in the end to be blamed for their anger. But as adults we quickly realize that this happens everywhere. We only have to watch young parents on the street. Usually, however, we have no access to the feelings this kind of behavior should arouse (memories).

(*1 June* 2006)

The Power of Repression

Of course, you have repressed most of what you've been through. If you hadn't, you would not have survived that hell. But you don't need to go in search of countless memories. You are fourteen years old, your feelings are awakening, the way they always do in puberty, you have an inkling of what life has to offer. Then your mother comes along and warns you of the devil so as not to have to recall her own repressed traumas. In this way you and your vitality are sacrificed. And now you are repeating your mother's behavior, over and over again. You are making progress, you can feel the life you have within you. But you will not allow yourself to do so because you are still just as much a slave to the voice of your mother as you were when you were fourteen. With the help of this one memory, keep trying to work on the problem. You will see that the devil will not come to get you. Instead, you will banish him for good.

(9 June 2006)

Reducing Self-Blame

You seem to have come a long way, and you know a great deal about the story of the child you once were. This helps you to see all the connections. The more empathy you display for that child, the more likely she is to tell you with the help of your body and your dreams how dreadfully she suffered when she was forced to blame herself for all the ill-treatment she received and was not allowed to see who was really to blame. You will listen carefully to all these communications, and you will constantly have to remind the child within that she was a victim of abuse and that there is absolutely *no* justification for the cruelties inflicted on her. In this way, the child you once were will finally have an "enlightened witness" who can enable her to become a feeling adult.

(12 June 2006)

Fantasies

I can readily imagine that your fantasies provide you with a private space where you can develop your thoughts and sense your feelings without exposing yourself to the fears you were subjected to in reality as a child. This is a creative achievement, and it will give you the strength to face up to reality without fear in future, should this be necessary. To my knowledge there is no literature on this subject, but you can collect your observations, write them down, and later publish something of your own. At the moment your "intact world" is perhaps itself a kind of "helping witness" for you.

(*14 June 2006*)

Tomorrow's Perpetrators?

Your remarks are based on a misunderstanding. I have pointed out very frequently that in my view every perpetrator was once a victim. But this does not mean that every victim has to become a perpetrator. Only those who deny their childhood sufferings and play them down or sneer at them are in danger of becoming perpetrators. Those able to take their sufferings seriously do not need to avenge themselves on others. People who have received affectionate attention in childhood do not carry destructive potential around with them, they are not time bombs, they feel empathy for themselves and others. But since most of the torments suffered in childhood are unknown because they have been denied, and since childhood is often idealized, we sometimes hear it asserted that there are destructive people who had a good childhood. This I believe to be inconceivable. Only emotional awareness of what happened to us in childhood and empathy for the children we once were can protect us from the blind repetition of our own unconscious sufferings.

(*16 June 2006*)

A Miracle

I was shocked when I read the account you have sent me. It is no wonder that after such a dreadful childhood you should have suffered so much in your marriage and with your children. Once we have learned at a very early stage to put up with cruelty in silence, we continue to do so and consider this quite normal. The real miracle is that you have now seen through this system and that you can finally see, feel, and say what was inflicted on you. This is rare because, as I have often experienced, the severity of the cruelties done to us is proportional to our desire to defend our parents and understand them, hoping perhaps to earn their love in this way in spite of all. But you appear to have freed yourself of this compulsion. Though you may still experience setbacks, you have already achieved such a high degree of awareness that you will no longer be tempted by emotional bribery. I hope you'll have positive encounters in the future with people who have achieved the same awareness as you have and have overcome their child-hood fears, at least in part.

(17 *June* 2006)

What Should I Do?

You write: "He changes her diapers and wants me to watch." Per-haps this is a more or less conscious plea for help. What stops you from telling your brother what you have observed and asking him whether he knows that these sexually tinged "games" with his daughter's body will have severe lifelong consequences for her? Is it conceivable that her life is just as indifferent to him as his own was to his parents? A child is not a toy; a child is a person whose dignity must be respected. Today ignorance of this fact can get a person put in prison. Your brother's reaction will tell you whether you should bring a charge against him or whether you can expect him to change his ways.

(19 June 2006)

Why So Few?

When did people start abusing their children? I do not know. In the 1980s there was a spate of feminist publications full of accounts of an early matriarchal community in which there was allegedly no violence and everyone lived together in peace. I have no way of knowing whether this is true, but today I see that, in terms of violence, women are no less guilty than men. Unfortunately, the people they are most likely to do violence to are babies and small children. Accordingly, the question that interests me is not the theoretical issue of what things were like earlier, but rather what I see *now*, and what other people prefer not to see because it causes them pain. Speculating about earlier times does no harm, but neither does it suggest any solutions for the damage done to children at a tender age. The idea that things were better in the "old days" stems perhaps from our childhood, a time when we found it impossible to believe that people can be so cruel to such tiny creatures. This made us hark back to better times. I do not know whether they actually existed. Was there ever such a place as Paradise? And if there was, why did God set up such cruel commandments in that Paradise? Why should human beings not eat from the tree of knowledge?

(20 June 2006)

Mental Blockades

Today there are so few people who do not take pills, smoke cigarettes, or drink alcohol. Most of them resort to these things to achieve an artificial state of well-being that can divert their attention from unpleasant thoughts, rather than prompting them to try to understand them. So how can they appreciate their true meaning or even try to? How can they realize that these feelings are their true friends, attempting to put them on a track that would lead to self-knowledge? Experience is the only thing that can bring this home to them. You have had this experience, and now, to your astonishment, you find that the quality of your life has definitely changed for the better. But you will not be able to explain this to someone in the grip of the products manufactured by the pharmaceutical industry. They will not be able to listen to you. They will carry on "loving" their parents until they run into a crisis and suffer from depression or attacks of panic fear or both. But there are allegedly "effective" remedies for that as well. Extreme intelligence is no safeguard. These people will use those remedies as a drug to help them deny their own truth. Why do they do this? Because they are driven by the panic fear felt by the children they once were at the prospects of more beatings if they should dare to see the truth or speak out about it.

So all I can say in response to your question about why so few people want to uncover their own histories is that the overwhelming majority of people in this world were beaten in *early* childhood.

(22 June 2006)

An Attempt to Explain the Origins

To small children, their parents are omnipotent, omniscient, loving gods. Invariably. If they experience things that contradict this view, if their loving father shouts at them and hits them, then they will try to "explain" this by blaming themselves in an attempt to salvage the immaculacy of the gods they need to survive. In my view, this infant strategy perpetuates itself in the attempts by theologians, and also many philosophers, to preserve the childlike image of God. Why did the loving Father sacrifice His son and let him be crucified? To redeem us from our sins. Why did He forbid us to attain knowledge immediately after Creation (birth) and *before* any "sin" had been committed? Certainly for our own good. We do not need to understand His motives because we believe in His love. Why does He permit wars, child abuse, and senseless murders if He is omnipotent and could therefore help us? Because we are evil and deserve no better. One could carry on this vein and make a nice fable out of it. But it has nothing to do with the reality of a feeling human being who does not need to live with obvious contradictions.

(22 June 2006)

You Cannot Please Everyone

Telling a child in nursery school that he is to blame for his caregiver's stomach ulcer is unconscionable. Perhaps this caregiver had to tolerate this kind of assertion in silence as a child so as not to risk punishment. But you do not need to please colleagues like this because you know what you are doing and the reactions of the children will confirm that you were right to do so. If you side with the children, you may well be attacked by your colleagues. But you will know why, and your knowledge will give you the strength not to be deflected from your path. I wish you the courage to stand by your own feelings.

(29 June 2006)

Allergies

Actually, you have already provided the answers to the questions you ask me. Obviously there are emotions that you are not yet able to admit to, perhaps because they are too painful or because you are afraid of saying no and running the risk of losing someone (as you graphically illustrate yourself). But then your body will say no in the form of an allergy, and it will no longer need to do this once you let those feared emotions live. After all that you have achieved so far, you will definitely be able to do this at some point. Take your time. Having yourself desensitized is probably counterproductive. After all, it is your regained sensitivity that has guided you to a clear-sighted view and to new health. The allergy is the language of your body. As soon as you manage to understand it, the allergy will disappear.

(4 July 2006)

My Life

Your childhood was terrible, and of course you now urgently need an "enlightened witness" who will stand by you with his indignation and display his true feelings instead of concealing them behind a routine mask of neutrality. But psychoanalysts' training does not allow them to do this, which is why you quite rightly sense that this cannot be the path for you to take. Your description and your criticism of the situation are completely clear and absolutely plausible. You ask me what you should do, but at the same time you add: "Whatever happens, I shall have to stay with this analyst because otherwise my health insurance will not pay for my treatment." This sentence reminds me of a story someone told me years ago. A person is walking down a dimly lit street at night and sees a man looking for something under a lamppost. Asked whether he needs help and what he is looking for, the man replies that he has lost his spectacles. "Are you sure you lost them here?" the other person asks. "No," is the reply, "I may have lost them further down the street, but it's dark down there, so I can only look for them here, where there's more light." This story illustrates the situation of all children dependent on the understanding, love, and respect of their parents, though all they ever get from them is exploitation, humiliation, and physical cruelty. But they never stop waiting for love from people who are incapable of true affection. They have no choice. They do not know that there is anything else but abuse (which they cannot recognize as such). But adults are not dependent on self-deception and the belief that there is no other path they can take. Alternatives always exist, once one is prepared to see how one was deceived as a child and resolves not to be treated in this way any longer. Your insurance company may be playing the role of your parents or the lamppost. It is there to "serve" you. But the "services" of your parents did you severe harm, and one day you will have to feel the anger this has aroused in you. If you can find someone to assist you with empathy for your anger, you will discover the possibilities open to you and relinquish the attachments that have forced you to deceive yourself. Your letter proves that you are capable of seeing the truth of your childhood, step-by-step, that you no longer want to tolerate, play down, or understand the cruelties inflicted on you.

(*6 July 2006*)

Blind Man's Bluff

I am very glad to hear that you can make use of my books in your practice. How much confusion and new suffering could be avoided if doctors were prepared to inform themselves of the *causes* of illness. Sometimes one conversation with a patient would suffice to set the healing process in train. Only the body has these healing powers, not medication. If a doctor were merely to ask a person suffering from asthma, an allergy, a stomach ailment, or a skin disease about their childhood—for example, whether they were beaten or tormented in other ways—then in most cases the truth would come to light, unfiltered, a truth that has been waiting to communicate itself for decades. This would immediately cast light on the whole development of the symptoms and on the early feelings of helplessness that the patient has been fearing all this time, although the reasons for it no longer exist. But doctors shy away from such questions, preferring to prescribe all kinds of medication designed to suppress and camouflage bodily knowledge. The pharmaceutical industry does the rest. Countless advertisements for Valium, Viagra, and antidepressants pop onto our computer screens every day, thus pulling the wool over the eyes of millions. These dupes are all people who suffer from the effects of their own childhood. They are not allowed to know what they are suffering from because society avoids this issue like the plague, and the experts in the health system all take part in this game of blind man's bluff. If a man is suffering from impotence, his body is telling him that he is repressing strongly negative emotions against one particular woman, or against women in general, or against his mother, although he believes he loves her. As soon as he can actively experience those "negative" feelings and identify the reason for their repression, his impotence will disappear. But if he takes Viagra, he will move further and further away from his feelings, and finally he will be confronted by other symptoms as well. He will be caught up in a vicious circle, instead of pausing to ask himself the necessary questions. Doctors *could* do a great deal to help *if* they were prepared to ask questions about their own lives.

(7 July 2006)

Self-Help Groups for People Abused in Childhood

The idea that a self-help group could help you discover little A. and grow to love her seems quite right to me. I cannot understand how you can have been undergoing therapy for five years but only realized a few months ago that you were an abused child. What were you doing in those five years? My impression from your letter is that you now know precisely what you are looking for. You know what you are after, so you will realize very quickly whether a group is right for you or not. If it is not, then you can try another one. You need not fear that you will stop "functioning" if you get closer to your own personal truth. We do not come into the world to function, but to live. For this we need contact with our own histories, our early emotions, and our roots. Once you learn to understand your feelings, you will understand your husband and your son better. I wish you the strength to achieve the goals you have set yourself.

(17 July 2006)

Neglect

You write: "I have not always had a positive perception of my parents and the circumstances of my life. But looking back, I find it necessary to admit that my parents were always good to me, benevolent and helpful. The fact that I was unable to perceive this for so long was not the fault of circumstances but of my own perception. I have never taken a positive view of others and the things around me. Accordingly, I have always felt them to be alien and threatening."

Obviously, you see your mistrust as an error on your part and not as the consequence of treatment that made you mistrustful. This view of things appears to help you, and it is not for me to correct you.

Instead, I should like to thank you for your important contribution. In the course of this correspondence I have obviously failed to make it clear that I consider neglect of a child and of its need for closeness and stimulation in the early years as a form of mistreatment. You are absolutely right to point out that the first few months have a very decisive influence. This is the time when so-called "primal trust" should normally form. In the parents' absence it can hardly do that.

(18 July 2006)

The Abandoned Child

When a child is abandoned, his very existence is threatened. He cannot help himself, and his psychic integrity is also in danger if he has to distort himself, repress his true emotions (rage and despair), and keep smiling to earn the affection of others. This generates a great deal of fear. Perhaps the *reason* you can feel this now for the first time is the fact that as an adult you are no longer exposed to this danger. You are no longer forced to please others; you can admit to, and display, your true feelings, but only to people who can do the same and are open and frank with you. If you feel that this is not possible, that others are afraid of your own true self, then you will also sense the existential fear of the child that was forced to give himself up in order to be "loved." This is only too understandable, but perhaps this fear will go away if you remain true to your feelings and try to understand them. This is something an abandoned child cannot afford to do. But an adult can. Adults can never again be abandoned in this way, as long as they remain true to their own selves.

(*24 July 2006*)

Abuse Real or Imagined?

You write: "When I was small, I was asleep in my bed when my father hit me with his belt, waking me up by doing so. Since then, I have always been an apprehensive sleeper. I still have no idea why he hit me. He used to throw shoes at me and my sister. He stood guard over us when we were doing our homework, and if I made a mistake he would hit me on the back of the head." This makes it obvious that you were a severely abused child. You can only free yourself of the consequences if you have *no more doubts about the fact*. But you appear to be a long way from this goal, which is why you let your "boyfriend" still treat you as if you were a defenseless child. But you are not. You are an intelligent adult woman, but your fear and denial make it impossible for you to realize that. This is clearly expressed in your next hesitant sentence: "Now I *ask* myself whether this image of men that manifested itself in my mind all those years *might* (!!!) have something to do with my father and my childhood. All my ex-boyfriends were drug-dependent, aggressive, in prison, or psychotic. They all treated me badly, then put the blame on me and left me." These two quotes show that you are fully aware of your situation but are still afraid to express the truth because unconsciously you still expect the blows of your brutal father or the boyfriends who resembled him. But you no longer need expose yourself to such dangers. It is up to you to leave a man as soon as he displays features similar to those of your father. However, to do that, you must take your knowledge about both your parents *absolutely seriously* and no longer evade it. No such dangers threaten you today unless you expose yourself to them in order to preserve the flattering image of your parents.

(26 *July* 2006)

A Childhood without Witnesses

You had an appalling childhood. It is distressing to think that there was no one who could confirm the fact, so that you have been constantly deceived on this point. But now you have hit on the idea of writing to me, and when we publish your letter, you will have many empathic witnesses who will express their indignation at your mother's behavior. With this letter you have resolved to become your own "enlightened witness," and this is the best thing you could have done. You describe your childhood very clearly in a way that invites empathy, but your anger and bitterness at so much brutality, hunger for power, and stupidity still appear to be blocked off. This is hardly surprising. You had to suppress these strong emotions for so long because there was no one to see your plight in the prison guarded over by a severely disturbed mother. Now you have perceived them, and I hope that your therapist can help you live out the strong emotions you were unable to admit to earlier. You have the gift of clear expression; do not let anyone take that away from you. It verges on a miracle that you should have seen through the tissue of lies woven by your mother. You can only help yourself with the courage to see your own truth. I wish you the same clarity of purpose in the future.

(30 July 2006)

How Can I Tell My Parents about My Sufferings?

On no account should you try to talk to your parents. Your body has quite rightly warned you not to do so. We cannot expect people who had so little compassion for their child to become wiser or more humane with age. Your father still displays the same malevolence at the age of ninety. It is right for your body to rebel against such an exchange and to protect you from new injuries. Take its warnings seriously!

In your childhood there was no one to see how you were suffering. Accordingly, your body was forced to develop a symptom to draw attention to your distress, but this was all to no avail. Now you understandably want to write about it and make your parents look your way—at long last! But they are unlikely to do that. Everything you write indicates that they are still as impervious as ever. What you might do is write to the little girl you once were, thus becoming the enlightened witness she so sorely missed. Write to her everything you can remember, tell her how terrible it all was. Ask her how she felt when she was forced to apologize after receiving another beating. Use this dialogue to reveal all the brutality you were exposed to, admit to your feelings of rage, and let yourself respond with horror to this inhumanity. It may be that the symptom will be temporarily aggravated by your arousal, but in time it will almost certainly disappear once you give expression to your indignation and stay in contact with yourself as a little girl. If you give that child someone to talk to, she will no longer need to express herself with physical symptoms. She can use words that only you will hear because you *want* to hear them and be receptive to them.

(*2 August 2006*)

Overcoming Fear

You write: "I have the impression that I create problems where none exist. I feel badly when I see the problems other people have to deal with and compare them with the trivialities I rack my brains over." Who is saying this? Have you identified so completely with your parents' viewpoint that you are prepared to play down your childhood sufferings without noticing it? If writing does you good, try writing to the little girl you once were, asking her how she felt when she was slapped in the face. Can she remember how she was soundly "spanked"? I believe that this might help you get in touch with the strong emotions that are still blocked off. The reason I believe this is the fact that you so obviously want to do so. The fact that this wish is interfered with by your fear of your parents need not surprise us; it is quite normal. But you seem to have gone in search of yourself, over and over again, so one day you will overcome that fear. I wish you every success in your future attempts.

(*3 August 2006*)

Dreams instead of Memories

You write: "Try as I may, I have no memory of actual cruelty. But I have terrible dreams that have frequently dogged me for years at a stretch." But your dreams *are* your memories. In a highly ingenious way, and with rare clarity, they are telling you what you had to bear as a totally dependent child, something you did not want to know for decades (no cruelty!). In contrast to your assertions, your dreams are obstinately telling you about the constant threats, the monstrously exaggerated demands, and the unending deception you were subjected to. You need no longer rack your brains for concrete memories; your body obviously knows the whole story. What you have yet to acquire is compassion with the little boy who was given the job of saving his parents at the cost of his own life (genuine feelings). You have yet to feel the boundless indignation at parents trying their best to foist their serious perversions onto their child and alienating him from his own heart in the process.

But now your true feelings (rage and disgust) do appear to be making themselves felt. They are still muted, hesitant, and fearful (not without reason, of course), but they are authentic. That gives you the chance, as an adult, to win back your own "heart." Merely by writing this letter you have abandoned your loneliness and the silence imposed on you. You have told your story to other empathic people and you have started to find your way out of the mendacity and the denial the intelligent child was forced to live in, for all his intelligence. Thanks to your dreams, you have started to see your life in a clearer light.

(5 August 2006)

I Have What It Takes

You write that despite your terrible childhood you are now able to live the way you always wanted to, that you have freed yourself of your guilt feelings, and are also able to admit to feelings of anger when the situation warrants that, above all anger at your parents. This liberation is quite definitely attributable to the fact that you no longer need to fear your parents as you did in childhood, nor do you need to sympathize with them as most people do, because you have the courage to see how they treated you. But where did you get the courage to trust your perceptions rather than allowing yourself to be confused, as is the case with almost all abused children? Might it be that, as a child, you were not alone with your knowledge because you received support from older siblings who also suffered seriously at the hands of your parents? Your brother's suicide may be an indication in this direction. What do you think of my conjecture?

(6 August 2006)

Brother as "Enlightened Witness"

The sincere love and care provided by your brother (your "enlightened witness") rescued your integrity, by which I mean your ability to recognize your mother's cruelty and to engage with its consequences at a later stage. Abused children without witnesses have no choice but to put up with even the worst conceivable tortures, to believe them to be normal, indeed to interpret them as signs of love and affection because they have no opportunity for comparisons. I believe neither in miracles nor the devil. Everything has its causes, good and evil alike. In these unfortunate circumstances you were lucky.

(9 August 2006)

Silent Tears

It is a good thing that you can paint. Much will reveal itself to you of its own accord. Do not try to find anything specific (this never happens intentionally). Just see what you come up with by simply enjoying the activity of painting. This is no contradiction to the tears it is bound to produce. Those tears can be a profound relief for you because they will help you get in touch with your true feelings and emotions. Colors arouse the strongest emotions.

(17 August 2006)

Political Immaturity

Unfortunately, physical "correction" of children did not cease after the war. Most people still consider it a suitable method of bringing children up and are completely unworried about the consequences of such treatment. They blithely tell others of the "good hidings" they received (because this is allegedly quite "normal") and insist that such beatings were "good for them." One striking thing about some discussions is that no one inquires how those people who voluntarily threw in their lot with the Hitler regime had been brought up. Accordingly, the assumption still prevails that "normal" parenting cannot do any harm. In discussions about the naïveté of young people signing up for national service of their own accord (this happened in the First World War as well), it is frequently remarked, quite casually, that they were "hardly any more than children." Obviously, we prefer to forget that political blindness affected not only young people but millions of adults, including writers like the German playwright Gerhart Hauptmann and philosophers like Martin Heidegger. I believe that, almost without exception, those millions were so cruel because they had

had obedience drilled into them by physical punishment, This kind of upbringing bore fruit. As adults, these abused children were unable to identify the cruelty of Hitler's plans. Some unconsciously took advantage of this opportunity to avenge themselves on scapegoats for the insane punishments inflicted on them by their parents, thus turning into active persecutors of innocent people. Others remained passive and swam with the current. Unfortunately, only very few people permit themselves to understand this dynamic. Abused when they were young, they still fear horrendous punishment if they allow themselves to identify the cruelty of their own upbringing and feel the sufferings of the helpless children they once were. As long as they deceive themselves and believe that they deserved those thrashings and that their childhood was "quite all right" in that respect, they need not expose themselves to fear. Today old men who had signed up for the SS when they were young are sometimes upbraided for their connivance. But no one ever asks them: "How did you feel in your parents' home? Were you allowed to defend yourself against absurd punishment? Were you in fact allowed to identify its futility and cruelty? What makes you so afraid of admitting to something that may have been the consequence of your upbringing rather than your own free will? Was your whole upbringing geared to teaching you obedience rather than allowing you to decide for yourself?" Thus everything that happened prior to puberty remains in the dark. We often seem to think that life begins at the age of fifteen. Although childhood can tell us so much that might wake us up, it is a subject passed over in silence. But in fact it is a mine of information that needs to be unearthed if we want to preserve ourselves from the future consequences of politic naïveté and blindness. Today this is more necessary than ever.

(*19 August 2006*)

Illness as a Way Out?

Yes, if there is no other way out, an abused child will express himself by means of illness. Luckily, you see the connections and do not deny the pain inflicted on you in childhood. This is rare in cancer patients. But you tell me that you cannot establish contact with your anger. Try to imagine that you are sitting at table, at your present age, with two giants who keep stuffing something into your mouth. They tell you that you will die if you don't swallow it. You believe them because they're armed. You don't want to die, so you gag and swallow the disgusting stuff, cod-liver oil and all. Perhaps now you will be able to feel your rage and stop sparing your parents, who exposed you to such torments without the slightest compunction.

The tragic thing is that you have been forbidden to express your anger. This fear of your parents has made you ill because you were cut off from your strong emotions for so long. But now you have the chance to regain your health because you are looking for your anger, and I have no doubt that you will find it. The reason why I am so confident is that today there is no more punishment threatening you, as long as you are prepared to *know* and *feel* how inhumanly you were treated by your parents. Your illness must surely leave you in no doubt about the fact—or am I wrong?

(*27 August 2006*)

Who Is Perverted?

I am glad that your dreams are trying to guide you. In my view, the child on your lap is no one other than *you*. It is wonderful that you want to care for him, that is all you need to restore your health.

But you are constantly interrupted in this important task by the perversity of your mother, whom you still believe like a little child. The shards of glass you spit out are your mother's lies and distortions of the facts. In your waking life you cannot see through them for fear of punishment. But in your dreams you keep on spitting out this poison. The truly perverted element in your life is your mother. You have always had to swallow this poison, right from the start of your life. Now you will have to keep on vomiting until all her lies, warnings, and intimidations have been expelled. Then you will stop believing all this rubbish and devote your attention to the child telling you clearly who you are and where you belong, and that you are not alone in your search. There are other people looking for their own truth, but you will only find yours when you have the courage to see that what you thought to be inconceivable was in fact *real*.

(*2 November 2006*)

Questions from a School Class

1. *What treatment of children is likely to cause traumas?*

   Lack of respect, emotional exploitation, ignoring the child's feelings and needs, beatings, creation of fear, contempt, derision, and much more.

2. *What does traumatization actually involve? And how does this manifest itself in children's behavior?*

   In nursery school and later at school, children traumatized at home will display the destructive patterns they have learned at home. Either insecurity and fear will be apparent, or the child will hide those feelings behind aggressive behavior. Both alternatives will be assessed by unempathic teachers as indications of disobedience and troublemaking. They will respond with punishment that causes even more fear. Teachers with the courage to see the parents' abuse, to talk to them about it, and explain the disastrous and frequently lifelong consequences for the child are quite rare.

3 *How can experts and laypersons identify traumatic events from the behavior displayed?*

They are easy to identify, provided we actually want to see them. But if we fear our own repressed memories, then we will look away and tend to resort to punishment. But this only reinforces the fears (see question 2 above).

4. *Who can one turn to when trauma has occurred?*

There are many youth welfare offices and similar institutions, but I know of none that side unequivocally with the children. The people working there are usually so afraid of their own parents that they try to make the abused children understand their parents' deeds and instill guilt feelings into them, rather than protecting them from incomprehensible cruelty. Children cannot understand that the sole reason for the cruelty inflicted on them is that their parents deny the torments of their own childhood, idealize their parents, and unconsciously repeat that behavior with their children.

5. *What can relatives or people in the child's immediate surroundings do to help?*

It is very rare for people from the children's social environment to have the courage to show them that they are being used as scapegoats. But that would be a decisive gain for the future. Otherwise these children will feel guilty and later, as adults, avenge themselves on their own children, again unconsciously.

6. *Are there effective countermeasures against the traumatization of children? And if so, what are they?*

Children need respect, protection, affection, honesty, understanding, and a great deal more besides. Taken together, this is what we call love. But parents who have never received love and were forced to interpret cruelty as love can give it neither to themselves nor to others, unless they have realized later that the treatment they received was not love. Recognition of one's own truth stands at the beginning of a process of awareness and engenders the awakening of empathy and an ability to love both oneself and one's children.

7. *What do you expect people in a child's environment to do to ensure, as far as possible, that traumatization cannot occur?*

It would be helpful for the parents of newborn babies to receive organized visits from people who do not deny their own truth and can show the parents what their child needs. You can learn empathy, but only if you have someone to model yourself on. Friends proffering good advice in an attempt to "correct" the child cannot provide such knowledge. Young parents urgently need to be enlightened on the *reasons* why they might feel the urge to maltreat their children. On my Web site we intend to organize a telephone service for despairing mothers who are tempted to beat their children. They would need to be told on the phone that the anger they feel at that moment is not directed at the child but at their own parents, who humiliated them and made them helpless without ever allowing them to defend themselves in childhood. This anger may materialize in the face of their own children, but it must never be yielded to because this will have serious lifelong consequences. What the newspapers keep on telling us is not true. It is not lack of time, stress, or poverty that generates abuse and hard-heartedness. Only denial of the torments experienced in childhood produces violent and ignorant parents.

(6 November 2006)

Jehovah's Witnesses

You write: "I find it very difficult to fathom my deepest feelings. It is as if there were something blocking me off from them, so I make very little progress. Sometimes it goes so far that I have no confidence left in myself and cannot assert myself at all." In this you share the fate of countless individuals who have experienced similar things, particularly if they grew up in a cult. But what distinguishes you from such people is the clarity of your memories and your awareness of the immense and terrible wrongs that have been done to you. Now it is essential to feel your own revulsion at all the crimes committed on that small, helpless, and innocent girl who had no one to turn to for protection. You must allow yourself this indignation and go in search of people who will share it with you. Psychiatrists normally do not do this; they prescribe medication to tranquilize you instead. But the effect is counterproductive. When you are fully aware of the extent of those horrors, you should not be tranquil. You have been tranquil for long enough because you had no alternative. Only now can you start listening to your body and defending its rights. You can give it your love and your understanding for its anger, which is absolutely justified.

You should take your "negative" thoughts seriously and listen to them. Those thoughts come from *within yourself*, they are telling *your story*. How can you expect to live an enjoyable life if you accept without protest that an attempt has been made to obliterate you? Now you are at a point where you have started to rebel against such oblivion, and initially this is probably very tiring. This is a beginning. If you want therapy, then please read the FAQ list first (see chapter 14, "How to Find the Right Therapist"). I wish you courage, and I hope that despite your fears and your experiences of cult terror you will find the strength to defend yourself against absurdity and crime.

(*15 November 2006*)

Confusion from Therapy

You ask: "Can one achieve one's integrity at any age, find oneself beautiful and worthy of living, even if one is ugly?" Yes, you can, at any age, provided you are determined to take your own feelings, memories, and dreams seriously and not let yourself be put off the track by clueless therapists. You have clear memories of revulsion at your stepfather and your mother. This is your truth, and your therapists have been trying to talk you out of seeing it as such with psychoanalytic interpretations. Hence your guilt feelings. Your body gives you important information and signals. Let yourself be guided by them. You have been told that you are ugly, and you think of yourself that way because you do not admit to your true feelings. Once you can do that, you will discover your beauty. You write: "My desire is, at least once before I die, to have been myself, just once, to feel and know what it is like. . . . I have no one I can talk to about it. . . . Former friends and the therapists I consulted all said that I am impossibly idealistic, that I am living in a dream, that I should wake up. What I want simply does not exist." Nonsense! Of course it exists. Everyone has the right to be themselves. Whatever age you are and however severely you were abused and humiliated in childhood, you have the chance to rebel, to feel your anger, understand it, and allow it to express itself so that you can eradicate the traces of the crimes perpetrated on you. Childhood is not just a stage in life, it is the *basis* of our whole existence. You cannot "get rid of it." But you can integrate it and become aware of it. In my view this is something we *must* do if we do not want to remain ill and continue to suffer. I wish you the courage to want to *see* your childhood.

(*3 December 2006*)

Torn Apart: My Life or My Parents'

Where do you get this idea that the lives and the happiness of your parents are only assured if you make yourself *unhappy and ill* and *refrain from leading your own life*? Is this some kind of law? Was this absurd and abominable responsibility imposed on you so early that you have never dared to free yourself of it? Now, fortunately, you appear to have had enough of it. Your letter indicates that you are still full of expectations that cannot be fulfilled. This is why it hurt you to send it. How can people who have never shown any understanding for you over the last twenty years suddenly be able to do so? I presume that you will sleep better and start enjoying your food if you decide not to send the letter and see how your body reacts. You are much too intelligent to continue putting up with so much hypocrisy without staying ill as a result. In fact, your body displays enormous vitality and strength by making you suffer so much for your attempts to adjust to what you call "smarminess." Listen to it, it is the voice of the little girl tormented first by her parents and now by you. Why should you play down her sufferings? Because religion tells you to? I cannot imagine a God who would demand that of you and still call himself merciful.

(17 December 2006)

Shaking Off Your Parents

You can shake something off that you have and know, but not something you have no knowledge of. Parents we have never looked in the face because we were afraid to do so can frequently ensconce themselves in our hearts and bodies. Finding them there and *then* freeing ourselves of them is no easy task. Perhaps you can take advantage of the fact that your parents are still alive and allow yourself to see them with the eyes of an adult doing her best to understand the child she once was. You appear to know next to nothing about your sufferings as a child.

(19 December 2006)

Unfeeling

You write: "Can you advise me how to get back out of this dilemma? I see it as an advance that I can actually feel grief, because earlier I was quite unfeeling." You had to be unfeeling in your early life, and now you can grieve for the child you were. So that child has much to tell you. Why do you want to abandon her again? Why do you want me to help you "get back out"? It would be irresponsible of me to do so. I too see it as an advance that you are finally capable of feeling. Fear of your anger is of course understandable. You would have been beaten if you had defended yourself. But this fear will diminish in the course of time because you will feel assisted by your therapist. Trust your body. It will find the right time for the indignation and the rage you are fully entitled to.

(24 December 2006)

What Should I Do?

You are already doing a great deal of good just by acting *differently* from most conventional nursery-school teachers. They automatically behave in the way their mothers brought them up, because as children they never dared to question that behavior. It would have been too dangerous. But you have the freedom to cast doubt on absurd injunctions. You might ask, for example: "Why should a child of fourteen months learn to eat with the right hand? If she instinctively reaches for the spoon with her left hand, then perhaps she is left-handed. This is something we must respect, otherwise we will do harm. But even if the child were right-handed, why should she be forced to do something that makes no sense?" The work you are doing is extremely important. It is an attempt to constantly question meaningless behavior, thus shaking your young colleagues' certainty that their mothers were infallible. Perhaps in this way you can at least contribute to preventing the use of "poisonous pedagogy" in nursery school.

(26 December 2006)

Waiting

I cannot give a general answer to your question. You will have to see what compromises you are able to make and where you have to draw the line. Your body will help you to find that out. And you can trust it. If you want a relationship of the kind we expect from adults, then you have no right to demand abstinence of your mother. You must leave it to her to decide whether she wants to go on drinking or not. But of course you do not need to force yourself to put up with things that get on your nerves. As an adult, you are free. Only children cannot live without their mothers. As adults, this is something we can learn.

(27 December 2006)

Am I Harming Myself?

It is uncommonly painful and infuriating to experience the fact that, although we have been seriously harmed, no one will believe that this is the case, not even our own mother. This is so unsupportable that many people elect to blame themselves and doubt the authenticity of their own (physical!) experience. This can cause very severe confusion, sometimes culminating in schizophrenia. Luckily, you have not let yourself be confused. You see the dangers, though perhaps not the full scope of them. Accordingly, your question is entirely justified. Are you harming yourself by playing down your mother's guilt? You most certainly are. *Full empathy* is something you owe the little child you once were, not your mother. That child needs full and unequivocal partiality on your part.

(5 January 2007)

Literature

Thank you for your letter and the quotes you believe to have a rightful place under this heading "Readers' Letters." But in fact you are mistaken. These citations are literature. There you will find any number of descriptions of horrific childhood destinies. But as long as the authors present them as literature, the children in them can evade the terrible fear engendered by daring to see through one's own parents. Most of the letters printed here display that kind of courage. In my eyes this is *more* than even the finest literature; it is pure, unadulterated truth; it is life itself. I have never come across storytellers or novelists who are able to experience the sufferings of their protagonists as their own. Confronted by this question, they frequently react with raised eyebrows and insist that their products are fictitious. They do not want to admit to the pain of having been tormented by people they loved and expected love of in return. *We*, the readers, see the children they were when we read their books, but the authors themselves have difficulty in siding with those children and feeling their sufferings. They hope to "heal" themselves with literature. But in my view this hope is futile because the body has no part in the writing of stories. It remains an intellectual exercise.

(6 January 2007)

"Stop Crying, You Only Brought It On Yourself"

You tell the terrible story of your partner as if it were some unavoidable stroke of fate. It is not. Though such tragic stories happen in all cultures, to millions of people all over the world, they would be avoidable if daughters were supported in recognizing the poison that is making them ill. But they do not dare to, and society—therapists included—does not assist them to find out the truth but encourages them to stay blind. Your partner is paying a terrible price for this blindness; it has almost cost her her life and has certainly ruined her health because, as you write, "she does not want to lose her mother's love." But what kind of love is it that prompted her mother to look on for years as the child was sexually abused by her uncle and who now attempts to impose silence on her? You can only help her if she wants to help herself. Then you could show her how destructively she was treated by her mother and support her in breaking off all contact with her. As long as she remains dependent on her mother and is not allowed to see her as she is, *she is bound to remain ill.* Hospitalization or medical treatment would be futile. Could you overcome the effects of poisoning if you had to swallow a new dose of poison every day?

(16 January 2007)

The Torments of Self-Blame

Your mother has actually succeeded in ensuring that your genuine and entirely normal feelings continue to strike fear into you. She imposed extremely severe guilt feelings on you because that way she did not need to question her *own* behavior. This is tantamount to killing off the emotional life of a child. So it is no wonder that you sometimes hated your mother for that murder, particularly as you were entirely dependent on her as a child. But luckily you were still able to hate her occasionally and perhaps also sense that she deserved that hatred. This rescued your true self. There are people who are completely blocked off from feelings of that kind. Now you quite rightly want to get rid of your guilt feelings.

You can do that if you make it clear to yourself that your anger was totally *justified*. You can write letters to your mother without actually sending them, telling her what she has done to you and how terribly you have suffered as a result. In this way you can give your own self more room to grow, instead of letting yourself be abused to fulfill your mother's needs and corroborate her versions of the whole matter.

(18 January 2007)

Sexual Interference with Boys

Probably severe punishment would have been the result for you if you had seen through your mother's unconscious manipulations. She could not allow herself to see how destructively she was behaving toward you, and you have probably taken over this blindness from her. Her sadistic interference with your sleep has left its marks on you to this day. You were forced to go to bed early, then you were woken up in the middle of the night. Normal, uninterrupted sleep was the exception, not the rule, and this has never stopped tormenting you. But you describe these appalling cruelties as if it were not your own life you are writing about. There is no sign of justified anger. I hope that at some stage you will gain access to your understandable indignation.

(27 January 2007)

Loving the Child Within

You say that you do not want to expose the "child within" to any more dangers, that you want to protect her and give her your love, as well as full understanding. It is a major step forward when we stop abusing that child in the same way our parents did when we were small. I wish you (and that child) the courage and determination to carry on as you have begun. Even if you encounter setbacks, you will probably never forget how you felt yesterday when you wrote those two letters. This feeling will be your guide if you should ever stray away from the path you have embarked on and let yourself be tormented by the old guilt feelings that hurt the child within. Those letters are your promise never to leave that child on her own again.

(8 February 2007)

Hospitalization

Your questions are entirely justified. Aggressive dreams and fantasies are susceptible of understanding, particularly if we know the reason for them. Perhaps you could talk to the boy about those reasons? Try not to spare his parents, even if they are your friends, and do your best to take his sufferings completely seriously. Without your aid as an empathic witness, this is something he will hardly dare to do himself. No one at a psychiatric hospital will do that either. He will be given medication that will only exacerbate his profound confusion. I cannot say whether you will be lucky enough to find a wiser psychologist. Can your son talk to the boy about his childhood?

(13 February 2007)

Delusions

The picture you paint is alarming, but unfortunately it seems to be realistic. Present-day psychiatry appears to be laboring under the delusion that modern medication provides all the resources needed to drive out the demons of the past (the abuse suffered), both in patients and doctors. This leads to the grotesque denial of the causes of human suffering and also of fundamental *logic*. Unfortunately, I know of no hospital anywhere in the world where this is not the case, which of course does not necessarily mean that they do not exist. You will have to search. Luckily, you appreciate the logical connections. Might it be that your son's "psychosis" helps him to disbelieve his own traumatic experiences and hence to spare his father? Perhaps it would help if you and your husband told him how he was treated as a child and that unfortunately you have only now realized how wrong and presumably painful this was for him.

(13 February 2007)

Epigenetics—the Influence of Experience on the Genes!

I watched the program you refer to on television. I have not the slightest doubt that the first three to four years have the greatest impact on a person's character and emotional development, a process that begins at the prenatal stage. To understand this, we need to have got in touch at least once with the feelings of the little children we once were, children that may have grown up in an emotional vacuum or complete and utter horror. This is what I call torture. Only very few people are prepared to embark on such a journey into the heart of their own selves, and scientists are constantly devising theories to avoid the childhood factor and provide a genetic explanation for irrational behavior. As far as "epigenetics" is concerned, I consider it highly problematic to assert that the hunger suffered by the grandparents should have more impact on the lives of their grandchildren than the experiences of those grandchildren, either as the victims of beatings and other torments or as the recipients of love and respect. If extreme *affective* hunger dogs a child in its future life, then that is probably due to a family tradition of hard-heartedness and cruel treatment. It has nothing to do with the lack of food one hundred years ago. It is easier and more convenient to trace the causes back so far because this helps us avoid feeling our own pain. But that has nothing to do with scientific thinking; it is merely the flight from demonstrable facts.

(*25 February 2007*)

How Can I Tell My Daughter?

You have already done the right thing. You have told your little daughter the truth, and she has understood. This does not surprise me. Usually, children will understand readily enough if they are told the truth, unlike adults caught up in conventional thinking. People are now making you feel uncertain by trotting out the usual arguments ("every child needs a grandmother"—but why should this be so?). Part of your uncertainty may have to do with your desire for your mother at least to love this child, even if she could not love you. Such hopes are understandable, but they will quite frequently prompt a mother to leave her child with a grandfather who deserves the greatest mistrust and then to be horrified at the abuse he inflicts on her daughter. If the illusion had not been so strong, all this could have been prevented. It *may* turn out well, but the risk is too great to justify playing with fate like this. Trust your original feeling. Be guided by this feeling and your daughter's response, not what "people" normally think.

(*3 March 2007*)

Profound Gratitude and Inquiry

Incontrovertible facts indicate that you were marginalized by your family. Understandably, this both saddens and angers you. But your family insists that they did no such thing. They attempt to talk you out of your own perceptions and to blame you for being so sensitive. This kind of behavior suggests that as a child you were subjected to treatment of this kind for a long time. You tried to believe what you were told instead of trusting to your perceptions. This is how schizophrenia comes about. A child is forced to ignore his or her own perceptions and feelings. As a child you *were* helpless and at your wits' end. Now you are not. You *feel* you are at your wits' end because now—perhaps for the first time in your life—you are able to experience the feelings of the deceived child so intensely. It is a *good* thing that you can. Trust your feelings. Later they will show you the right route to follow. They will tell you what you *want* to do, whether you want to submit to your family's judgment or not. And you will act in the way that is right for *you*.

(7 March 2007)

Article on the Erasure of Traumatic Events by a Medicinal Agent

This is an interesting question. Will we be able to snuff out memories of traumatic events in humans in the same way we can with rats? And if we can, what good will this do? You ask whether this is not the same thing as repression. I believe it is. The fact is that we *easily* forget traumas. We do not suffer so much from conscious memories as we do from compulsive repetition and other symptoms produced by repressed, *unconscious* memories. In many cases it transpires that conscious awareness of the trauma in the *context of our own histories* can liberate us from our symptoms. Then the *significance* of the trauma is real and can be snuffed out for good. So how will "science" of this kind benefit us? Even more victims of tragic Alzheimer's disease? Would this be a consummation devoutly to be wished? People who want to know nothing about their own histories? We already have medication geared to the obliteration of painful memories. It is designed to combat depression, it works wonders, and many experts consider this the only solution. But many people could not find any meaning in their lives if they were separated from their own histories. Those histories give us the chance to understand our feelings and to behave in given situations in a way that helps us to find the ideal solution. How are we to find our bearings in life if we are only left with the good memories and we can never find out, say, why we suffer from headaches or stomach troubles? This would lead to extreme self-alienation. I fear that this idea of freeing people, like rats, from their unpleasant memories and thus "healing" them will catch on, particularly if the pharmaceutical industry gets interested in the prospect. But perhaps this has happened already and it is already investing money in such research.

(17 March 2007)

Feeling the Anger

Now it appears that the fears stored in your body are beginning to venture into your conscious mind, because at last you can afford to admit to them. As a child, you survived the horrors inflicted on you without being able to put a name to them. Now, as an adult, you have the chance to come to terms with them by feeling the appropriate anger and indignation. This is good. What we consciously feel and can give a name to no longer needs to express itself in physical symptoms.

(1 April 2007)

Religion, Christianity, Easter, Child Sacrifice

Thank you for your letter, which I agree with entirely. Unfortunately, opinions like yours are rarely voiced because anger is always felt to be a nuisance. The fact is, though, that repressed anger is a breeding ground for all kinds of illnesses. But neither physicians nor the majority of therapists wish to know that. Of course, the Crucifixion is an example of the sacrifice of a son, and the Old Testament is full of examples of this kind of mentality. All religions prize obedience to the parents as a supreme virtue. So what do we do with our repressed anger? Should we direct it at infidels (enemies) or take refuge in illness instead? It definitely cannot be eliminated, only directed at innocent victims.

(16 April 2007)

Poisonous Pedagogy in Primal Therapy

I heartily disagree with this theory and believe that it does indeed contain traces of poisonous pedagogy, compounded with Buddhist thinking, in which anger and rage are not allowed to exist. These *vital* and protective emotions are condemned by all religions, though to my mind they are the healthiest, most natural and logical reactions to the pain inflicted on us. Since children are not allowed to feel them, they have to be repressed (unlike sorrow, which is permitted). Neither in the family nor at school can they be felt and expressed in words. Accordingly, they have to remain trapped in our bodies and produce physical symptoms as a way of finding a hearing. If they are taken seriously in adult life and felt in therapy, the symptoms can go away because their sole purpose was to *rebel against injustice*, cruelty, perversion, mendacity, lies, and hard-heartedness. All this bitterness was locked up in the body. Now, in therapy, the hitherto forbidden emotions have to be experienced in the presence of a therapist who is not afraid of them. But if clients are made to believe that their anger is only a defense against sorrow and the illusion of "false power," then once again they will be prevented from admitting precisely this emotion into their conscious minds, an emotion that interferes with their bodily functions and that absolutely needs to be released for the sake of the adult's health. Obviously, such theories originate from the small child's fear of the next blow, a fear that lives on inside us and permeates so many therapeutic approaches, primal therapy among them. We prefer to be "good," obedient children and go on crying forever rather than becoming adult and feeling, and rebelling against, the endless injustice we were forced to bear in childhood. In my view this is precisely the risk adults must take.

(18 April 2007)

Poisonous Pedagogy from a Spiritual Perspective?

It appears to have become fashionable to use the word "spirituality" when therapists have become trapped in the blind alley of their own promises. I must admit that I have never understood the meaning or the necessity of this word that could so easily be replaced by others, once we try to think in concrete terms. When I read that authors agree with Buddhist or mystical thinking and understand spirituality as a feeling of communion with the universe, then I imagine the feelings of a small child punished and isolated by the family, then ultimately forgiven and reunited with the universe (the family). Fobbing off clients presumptuous enough to complain about abuse at the hands of their parents in childhood with vague, imprecise concepts may be a source of gratification for therapists still harboring feelings of guilt about their own anger. But in my view this is nothing other than deception, and certainly not a token of successful therapy.

(18 April 2007)

Denying the Child Within

Many people know nothing of the existence of the child within them because fear of their parents has always prevented them from hearing its voice and understanding its language. For this reason there are still many who neither share nor understand our discovery of the tormented child that communicates with us by means of physical symptoms and tells us of the sufferings it had to tolerate and experience. This voice is smothered by self-blame. To assert that no one can hear the child within and that it does not exist is like saying that everyone must be blind because we are blind ourselves. But you are beginning to see through this mechanism. The more successfully you do so, the more you will find out.

(18 April 2007)

Rage and Anger

I am so glad that you have recognized the significance of anger and rage. This realization is usually tabooed, notably in forms of therapy still influenced by poisonous pedagogy. These strong, liberating, and logical emotions are avoided until everything breaks down. No one can be healed if they fear their true and salutary emotions and understand them as something that prevents them from being "good." Clients are then frequently offered nebulous spirituality as a substitute for the inner vacuum, and everyone thinks they understand the word "spirituality" because they have been accustomed to manipulation since their childhood. They believe that anything is better than the simple truth that they were abused as children. This is why tremendous rage has been building up inside them. They can only free themselves of this rage by no longer denying its existence and by learning to see why it is justified.

(19 April 2007)

IV

INTERVIEWS

16

The Feeling Child

Interview, March 1987

Why do some professionals deny what you're saying?
Many consider my ideas alarming and dangerous, particularly if they feel obliged to see everything the way Freud saw it.

What is so alarming for them?
My references to child abuse and its consequences. A child's anger and the other strong feelings we had to fear are reactions to harm done in childhood. Today we know how often these things happen. The child is forced to repress the memory of this abuse, to deny the pain and the facts in order to survive. Otherwise he or she would die.

Might this happen so early in the child's development that he or she lacks words to express the pain?

That is true. But the pain was there all the same. The words have to be found in therapy. Good therapy should help the client evolve from a "silent child" to a "talking child." If the drama happened early and the environment was actively hostile, then the child could not have found those words. But now, in therapy, if you have a therapist who is really your advocate, a conscious witness of what happened to you in those early years, then the silent child will learn to speak. Therapy is there to help you find the words you need to tell your father or mother how you felt when you were still unable to say anything.

What do you mean by "advocate"?

One who sides with the child. Always. The therapist should not say that the parents were disturbed but well-meaning, because then he or she is siding with the adults. We cannot learn to feel—and particularly feel anger—if we are trying to understand and defend the people who hurt us. If children are made to think that the parents who humiliated them so cruelly were basically well meaning, then they will be unable to feel the pain and will become confused. They will sympathize and side with their parents. Battered children feel humiliated, confused, isolated. They are also made to feel guilty because they are told that they are bad. We are afraid to say outright that child abuse is a crime because we do not want to blame the parents. But we are not helping anyone by supporting their blindness, because in this way we are also betraying the children those parents once were.

How do you deal with pain in the healing process?

Pain is the way to the truth. By denying that you were unloved as a child, you will spare yourself some pain, but you will also block the path to your own truth. And throughout your life you will try to earn the love of your father and mother, because we all believe and hope that it has been there waiting for us since our childhood. After all, we are entitled to it, are we not? But this love we were hoping for as children is not waiting for us. It was never there, and it will never be there. However, as adults we can learn in therapy to love the children we once were. Most clients think it was their fault if they weren't loved. The feeling of guilt is a protection against the painful awareness that fate gave us a mother who was incapable of love. This is much more painful than thinking "she was a good mother but I was bad," because that is a situation we can do something about. We can do our best to earn that love. But you cannot earn love with "exploits" of any kind, and the feelings of guilt for what we have done or not done only reinforce our blindness and our illnesses.

In therapy it is important for clients to experience their feelings and express them in words. If they were badly treated as children and the therapist does not deny the fact, then they will open up, as long as the therapist does not preach forgiveness. That is counterproductive. Clients will then suppress their anger and vent it later on their children or other scapegoats.

Do you believe that children come into the world like a tabula rasa?

No, I don't. Children come into the world with the history they have been through in the womb. But they are born innocent and ready to love. Children are much better at love than adults are. My conviction on this point has run into so much resistance because we have learned to defend our parents and blame ourselves for everything they have done.

To what extent does your style reflect these views?

I try to reach the child in my readers and give them access to their feelings. I offer them an assortment of keys. Everybody can take one and open a door to their innermost being. Or they can say, "I don't want to open that door, you can have your key back." I try to evoke feelings with the help of images. Equipped with those keys, my readers can go to their children and learn more from them than they ever will from me. Because you can only really learn from your own experience.

Why did you decide to quit practicing and become an author?

I wanted to inform people about what I had found out as a therapist. I wanted to demonstrate that there is not one single person in the whole world who abuses children without having been abused as a child. Realizing this appeared crucial to me; it can help us to understand a great deal. As an analyst, I couldn't share this insight with my colleagues. It was impossible, and I wanted to find out why. Accordingly, I wrote my third book, *Thou Shalt Not Be Aware*. I felt very much like the child in Andersen's fairy tale who cannot understand why everyone else denies the most obvious facts, including the fact that the emperor has no clothes on. Then others began showing an interest in my work. The well-known anthropologist Ashley Montagu roundly confirmed my view, and I also received confirmation from other American authors writing about child abuse. Montagu sent me his book *Growing Young*, in which he sides unequivocally with my criticism of psychoanalysis. In it he quotes the famous British psychoanalyst Edward Glover writing about "ordinary" children and describing them as "egocentric, greedy, dirty, violent in temper, destructive in habit, profoundly sexual in purpose, aggrandizing in attitude, devoid of all but the most primitive reality sense, without conscience or moral feeling. Their attitude to society as represented by the family is opportunist, inconsiderate, domineering, and sadistic."

This view of children is highly dangerous for humanity. It is with ideas like this that experts believe they can enlighten children about social norms and make them into decent members of the community. It was a shock to me to see that this assessment of infants was based on psychoanalytic theories. This is strikingly apparent in the writings of Melanie Klein.

Have you had reactions to your books from Kleinian analysts?

This is rare. But a Dutch psychiatrist trained in the Kleinian school of thought once wrote to me: "What you have written seemed terrible at first and turned everything I had learned on its head. It scared me. But now I am grateful. Every day at the hospital is fascinating. I used to get cripplingly bored trying to discern the evil babies in people by peering at them through my Kleinian spectacles. Now I see the patient's histories, and I can learn from them."

When I say I'd like to open people's eyes and ears to the sufferings of children, this is very close to what Frédéric Leboyer did with newborn babies. So many people have witnessed births, yet none of them saw that the babies were crying because they were suffering. No one felt with the children. They were convinced it was necessary to cry after birth. Leboyer showed that this is not necessarily the case and that babies can smile only a few minutes after arriving in this world.

Professionals are rarely able to query what they have learned. What Leboyer did for newborn babies I try to emulate for infants by making their behavior understandable and thus preventing child abuse in the future. As long as we deny its existence, we cannot stop it. We just call it upbringing. I try to make adults aware of children's feelings, feelings that I first discovered in myself when I started to paint.

Has painting opened up your feelings for your own sufferings?

Certainly. I was unencumbered by theoretical considerations. I had so much fun when I started painting, something had been aroused inside me, something I had an inkling of but could not yet understand. After I had been painting for five years, I wrote *The Drama* without paying attention to the way other people wrote psychological books. It gave me the freedom to question many things I had learned from theory.

In The Drama *you connect repressed feeling with loss of vitality. Was that your own experience?*

Yes. Experiencing the pain of my childhood for the first time restored my vitality. The price for repressing our feelings is depression. For me painting, dreaming, and writing have something in common. I paint as I dream. Initially, I wanted to paint stories, now it's more like needing this color, this form, this line. It's more like an improvisation.

What are your thoughts about dreams?

Dreams tell me the story of childhood, but of course in an oblique way. The problems of the previous day are mixed in. Dreams frequently reveal the histories of traumas, but they also help the dreamer to master them. They are a creative force we all experience every night, when control relaxes. They can also be very helpful if we have a decision to make the next day because they sometimes tell us what we really want to do.

Can therapy effect a change?

It can, but only if it brings understanding of the pain that has been sealed off by guilt feelings. The idea that I am to blame for everything that has happened to me is a blockage. One can devise plenty of irresponsible and harmful techniques that trigger pain, but they do not help us to engage systematically with the past. Some therapists leave their clients alone with their pain. Those clients are victims first of child abuse, then of therapy abuse. Then they try to "help" themselves by taking drugs, joining sects, throwing in their lot with gurus, or various other ways of denying reality and killing pain. Political activity may be one of those ways.

What advice would you give today to a therapist embarking on training?

First, try to discover your childhood, then take the experience seriously. Learn to listen to your clients, not to theories. Forget them. Do not analyze the client like an object. Help him or her to find their childhood. If clients tell you about the sufferings inflicted on them (which is rare), always believe them. Believe everything they tell you, and never forget that repressed reality has always been worse than fantasies. No one invents traumas. They do not need them to survive. Nor do we need denial, although many think differently. Therapy should awaken your feelings for life as a whole. It should rouse you from a long sleep.

It is tragic for people to go for therapy and find confusion instead of help. Recently, I received a letter from a seventy-nine-year-old woman in which she says: "I spent forty years undergoing psychoanalysis. I saw eight different analysts. They were all very nice. But they never doubted that my parents had been good to me. After reading your books, I am so grateful that I no longer feel guilty. I see now how dreadfully I have been abused all my life, first by my parents, then by my analysts, where once again I felt that I was to blame for everything my parents had done to me. I was never allowed to believe my feelings, although they were telling me the truth the whole time." In her letter she quotes the last sentence from my book *For Your Own Good*: "For the human spirit is virtually indestructible, and its ability to rise from the ashes remains as long as the body draws breath."

Can society learn to understand the language of a child?

I hope so. Children's language is often very clear; it's just that we refuse to listen. Children may endure terrible abuse and cruelty from the very outset of their lives, not least thanks to the technology brought to bear on them in hospitals. The abuse is stored up in the brain and may remain active for a whole lifetime. Children maltreated by technology very quickly need someone to take them in their arms and tell them that the shock is over. Otherwise as adults they may spend all their time fearing a repetition and panicking on various occasions without knowing why.

One of the first lessons you learn is that you are alone in a dangerous place and no one takes any notice of your pain. But this situation can easily be changed, once we acknowledge that newborn babies are feeling and highly sensitive beings. Very often, children enter the world after quite a struggle, and we fail to realize that they need the consolation of their mother's arms. We give them medication, injections, and so forth instead, thinking that this is good for them, but only because we went through the same experience many years ago and believe that this is "normal."

A reader once wrote to me: "My mother was very concerned for my health and took me to see our doctor very frequently. But I cannot remember one single moment when I felt that she actually saw me, perceived me as a person. Not for one minute." To feel this defect, a person has to be aware of the need to be seen. But most people have repressed it at an early stage for fear of being punished for it.

What would you like to do next?

I want to support people who are working to heighten adult sensitivity to the sufferings of childhood. Children's advocates, rare though they are, can save lives by calling things by name. They do not hide the truth behind fine words. Such an advocate can save children from a life of crime. Children will learn to identify cruelty, reject it, and defend themselves against it. In this way they will escape the fate of repeating cruelty and inflicting it on innocent victims. Experiments have shown that no one can learn to love others by being punished. All they learn is how to evade punishment by lying. And it is in this way that they learn to maltreat their own children twenty or thirty years later. Despite these highly enlightening experiments, most people still believe that punishment can be productive.

What about milder forms of cruelty like spanking, shouting, or verbal humiliation?

The tragedy is that even people who have not been exposed to outright brutality and who have not turned into little Hitlers constantly insist that their "strict" upbringing was necessary. They claim the right to do the same things to their children and are dead set against a ban on physical "correction."

The ignorance in our society is the result of such "correction." We were beaten to make us blind. We have to regain our sense of sight if we want to give children a chance of growing up with more responsibility and more knowledge than our generation, which today seeks salvation in nuclear armament. Luckily, not all battered children later become dictators. But among those dictators I have not found one who was not severely abused in childhood.

17

Beyond Philosophy

Interview, November 1992

How would you describe your childhood?

I was the firstborn child of a typical middle-class family. My parents were much like anyone else. They were not alcoholics. They were not criminals. They even had the reputation of being good, concerned parents. But because they had not experienced love as children, but something more like neglect cloaked in hypocrisy, they had no idea what their duties to their children were. When their first child was born, they were aware of nothing but their own ungratified needs. With the help of that child they proceeded to try and fulfill those needs that they had been forced to repress in their own childhood: the need for attention, consideration, tolerance, respect, love, protection, care, and so forth. What that meant for me was that, from day one, I had to learn to repress my own needs.

In my early books I actually wrote a great deal about my childhood, albeit without realizing that it was my own experiences I was writing about. Since 1985, I have been doing so consciously, and therefore readers will find considerable autobiographical detail in my books. Various reactions over the past twelve years, from people with very different cultural backgrounds, have shown me that my childhood was in no way exceptional. The letters I have received indicate that similar destinies to mine can be found not only throughout Europe and America, but also in Australia, the Philippines, Japan, India, Vietnam, and many other countries. This was one of the reasons why I decided not to publish any further details about the places where I grew up. I did not wish my revelations about the repressed sufferings of childhood in general to be associated with my life, thus making it easy to dismiss them as "my personal problems." The tendency to do so is understandably great as uncovering one's own repressions is a painful process.

Experience has shown me that my decision was right. When people read my books, they come face-to-face with their own childhood. Often, it is the first time in their lives that their own story becomes important to them. And this is crucial. Before we have taken this emotional step, we know next to nothing about our own lives, even if we are aware of the facts. As I know from countless letters, my books have enabled some readers to embark on the discovery of their own histories without being distracted by mine. And I do not want to interfere with that effect.

Was there any particular moment or set of circumstances that prompted you to embark on what has proved to be your life's work?

Even as a child I asked myself: Where does human bestiality come from? Are people born as monsters? Can it be that newborn babies come into the world with genes that "make" them criminal?

Although our entire system of jurisprudence seems to be based on such a view of human nature, thus giving impetus to today's clarion call for the reintroduction of the death penalty, the notion of "inherent evil" has always seemed to me like the medieval belief in the devil and his children. Experience teaches us just the opposite. Studies have already incontrovertibly proved that all serious criminals were once mistreated and neglected children, children who early in their lives had to learn to repress their feelings, that is, to feel absolutely no compassion for themselves and, as a result, have no emotional access to their own stories. By becoming cynical, irresponsible, and brutal criminals they were able to hold their denial in place—but only at the expense of other people's lives. Today, I know—and in my books have tried to prove with ever greater clarity—that the destructiveness, and self-destructiveness, that dominate the world are not our fate. We produce them in our children, and the production of this destructive potential begins in pregnancy and at birth. An unwanted child's desperate struggle for the right to live begins in the womb, leading later to a loss of the capacity to love and trust others, and an inevitable inclination toward (self-)destructiveness. We can put an end to the production of evil as soon as we stop denying the proven facts and the knowledge we now have about childhood.

At the beginning of your career, were there any significant influences, mentors, models?

When I look back over my life, I can find no single person who might have supported, let alone accompanied, me on my journey toward the truth. My former teachers and colleagues clung obstinately to theories whose defensive character thus became increasingly clear to me. When I confronted them with the facts, they reacted with fear and incomprehension. My discoveries cast doubt on their theories, and they were determined, at all costs, to protect the name of Freud, so they simply chose not to understand what I was talking about.

Do you believe there is such a thing as "human nature"? If so, what do you think the quality of this nature is?

As I have already said, I regard all talk of death wishes, destructive drives, or genetically programmed evil as nothing but a flight from the facts—facts that have already been proven—and hence as self-inflicted ignorance. People who delegate their own responsibility to higher powers are willfully ignoring what the facts tell them. They don't care about the truth. They want to be left in peace. Goodness they attribute to God, evil to the devil or their children's innate wickedness. They also think that what they believe to be preordained can be transformed by discipline and violence. How could this possibly be the case? Has anyone ever come across one single human being whose "inborn" destructiveness has been transformed by beatings and other forms of mistreatment into good, positive character traits? Nonetheless, "scientists" still cling to their belief in the myth of "inherent evil," and millions of parents still go on mistreating their children in the belief that they can beat goodness into them. What they create instead is a submissive child, a child that may not reveal his justified anger today, but will later remorselessly act out his rage on others. The only ones who will not be forced to pass on this legacy of destruction are those who encounter, either in childhood or later, an "enlightened witness," someone who can help them feel the cruelty they suffered, recognize it for what it is and categorically condemn it.

And human nature? Ultimately, it is a philosophical question, though answers have never been forthcoming from philosophers, psychologists, or church reformers. Most of them were severely mistreated as children, but they repressed their pain, blindly defending, as mistreated children have done since the beginning of time, the very system that has made them suffer. Martin Luther, for instance, urged all parents to mistreat their children because he idealized the pitiless beatings his mother had given him and wanted to see them as something positive. In an attempt to transfigure the brutality he had been exposed to, Calvin, the reformer and spiritual father of the city of Geneva, wrote: "The only salvation is to know nothing and to want nothing . . . man should not only be convinced of his absolute worthlessness. He should do everything he can to humiliate himself." The philosopher Immanuel Kant put it this way: "Man has an inborn tendency toward evil. In order to prevent him from becoming a beast, this evil must be kept in check." Although these thinkers fly in the face of the demonstrable truth, their opinions are still taught at universities. For any feeling person, it would probably be enough to visit a maternity clinic and see what happens to newborn babies to realize what unnecessary suffering ignorance and pigheadedness can cause. A child will, for instance, be held up by the feet—so it can breathe, we are told—without anyone recognizing this as sadistic mistreatment. Since none of the people involved know what was done to them at the same age, the newborn baby's feelings will be totally ignored, despite the fact that today, with the help of ultrasonic technology, we can actually see that children already react to tenderness and cruelty in the womb. And they are not just reacting. They are learning. Society makes its first contribution to a person's potential for love or destruction right here, in the way it welcomes a new human being into the world. Upbringing can either worsen or greatly improve the situation. Everything depends on the capacity for love and understanding shown by the child's parents and other important people in his or her life.

Children come into the world with a whole bundle of needs. To fulfill those needs and experience respect, protection, care, love, and honesty, they are absolutely dependent on their parents. If those needs are not fulfilled and children are used, mistreated, and neglected instead, it is readily understandable that they will develop into confused, evil, or sick individuals. Evil is real. Hitler was real, so were his deeds. Who can deny that?

You seem to be suggesting that for many parents, raising a child becomes a kind of psychodrama in which their own mistreatment is reenacted in the brutalization of their child. That this happens with brutal child-abusers is well known, but what I would like to hear more about is how this re-enactment phenomenon affects the life of those millions of families whose inner workings do not go completely out of control but whose dynamic could nevertheless be called "abusive."

In fact, I have described precisely this dynamic in all my books, especially in *The Drama*. Like you, I thought that something as obvious as brutal mistreatment and its calamitous effects could not be disputed by anyone. With time, however, I came to see that even the most murderous attacks on a child can be made to seem harmless, often by the victims themselves. As children, they could not face the truth, and they continue to deny it as grown-ups, not knowing that they will no longer have to die of their pain. Only the child would have been killed by the truth and was therefore to repress it. Adults can relieve their repression. By experiencing the painful truth, they also have the chance of regaining their health.

What do you think the role of religion is in the raising of children? Also, how does religion affect the behavior of parents? I'm thinking particularly of how religion might affect the ideology of child-rearing?

People frequently draw my attention to quotations from the New Testament that emphasize the worth of children. But for many people, as we know, holding children in high esteem and sacrificing them is no contradiction. Indeed, the good faith and openness of children frequently tempt their emotionally starved parents to abuse and exploit them. Was Jesus himself not a particularly cherished son? But he was sacrificed all the same. In fact, I know of no religion that forbids and condemns the practice of child abuse. Respect, understanding, and love for our parents are universally preached, no matter how they behave. Children, on the other hand—according to Luther, for instance—should only be loved if they are obedient and God-fearing, that is, as long as they deny themselves. Parents have a right to the unconditional love and respect of their children. Dostoyevsky may have written in *The Brothers Karamazov* that a father should only be loved if he merits it. But he himself suffered from epilepsy because he was not allowed to know that he was also a severely abused child and the victim of indescribable brutality on the part of his father. Only thanks to his mother's love and help could he escape from becoming a murderer himself. But he could not escape his illness.

In one of my books I indicate how intelligent, religious-minded educators still advise people, as Luther did four hundred years ago, to use the rod today so that tomorrow the child "will be loved by God." In his important book *Spare the Child*, Philip Greven has shown how widespread sadistic and destructive methods of child-rearing still are, particularly those concealed under the mantle of religiosity. This is true not only of Christian child-rearing. One hundred million Islamic women living today have had their genitals mutilated as children. For the sake of dogma, millions of Jewish and Arab children are subjected to circumcision, either as infants or at a later stage. Such cruelty is only made possible by the total denial of a child's sensibility. But who can seriously say today that a child does not feel? In India millions of girls have been raped as "brides" in the name of the religiously sanctioned doctrine of marriage. Countless initiation rites condoned by religion are nothing other than sadistic mistreatment of children. Such scenes abound in many of the greatest paintings in the history of art, yet no one bats an eyelid. We have been brought up not to feel. As soon as individual human beings begin to feel, however, many things will inevitably change.

Some critics of the so-called "inner-child movement" have suggested that the concentration on childhood is a form of self-pity and even narcissism. How would you respond to this common criticism?

I do not represent any movement, so I do not know to whom exactly you are referring. Nor can I take responsibility for all that is, unfortunately, propounded in my name. I can only say in response to your question: Allowing the child inside us, whose integrity has been seriously damaged, to at last feel and speak, allowing it to discover its rights and needs is nothing other than enabling it both to grow and to grow up. Making feelings available to our consciousness means setting in motion a process of growth, assuming responsibility, and initiating a process of awareness. This process can only take place once we question parents and society as a whole, and once a person who has been blind to cruelty begins to see. I have never come across anyone in whom this process is not accompanied by genuine sympathy for, and interest in, others, nor anyone who does not wish to help others by communicating the knowledge they have gained. Of course, one can only help those who want to help themselves.

To my knowledge, all this is precisely the opposite of narcissism. The narcissist is trapped in his or her self-admiration and will not dare to venture on such a journey of self-discovery. The awakening of our own sensitivity to the things done to us as children enables us, for the first time, to notice what has been, and is being, done to others. This sensitivity to one's own fate is a condition—an absolutely essential condition—of our ability to love. People who make light of the mistreatment they received, who are proud of their imperviousness to feeling, will inevitably pass on their experience to their children or to others, regardless of what they say, write, or believe. People who can feel what happened to them, on the other hand, do not run the risk of mistreating others.

In the criticism that you mention I hear the voice of the submissive child, the child who was not allowed to see, feel, or grieve over its parents' unjust behavior and, instead, had to learn early on to regard all this as "self-pity" and despise it. But why should we not suffer from the suffering inflicted on us? What purpose would that serve? Is this not a shocking and extremely dangerous perversion of natural human *impulses*? We are born into the world as feeling beings. Feelings and compassion for ourselves are essential for us to find our bearings in the world. Isn't it bad enough to have been robbed of our capacity to feel, our compass for life, by blows and humiliation? When so-called specialists champion this perversion as a solution and preach "the courage for discipline," they should be unmasked for what they are: the blind leading the blind. Hitler was proud that he could count the thirty-two strokes his father once gave him without feeling a thing. Rudolf Höss and Adolf Eichmann made similar proud assertions. What that led to is common knowledge, though the connections have never been properly understood.

Some people would say that you tend to see the family in isolation, relatively unaffected by economics, culture, and history. How would you respond to this criticism?

That is precisely what preoccupies me more than anything else. In very different cultures, at very different times, under the influence of very different religions, I find the same thing: the abuse of children on a huge scale, accompanied by repression and denial. This phenomenon can be traced neither to a particular class nor to a particular economic system. Rich people can be child-abusers, or they can be loving parents. And the same goes for the poor. Only one thing is certain: people who were respected as children will later respect their own children. It is, after all, the most natural thing in the world. The reason that children are mistreated lies only in the repression and denial of one's own experience, something that the careers of dictators amply illustrate. I was told that there are cultures in which children are not mistreated and in which, significantly, no wars are fought. But I have no real knowledge of them. If you hear of such a society, I would be indebted to you for more detailed information about it.

18

Violence Kills Love: Spanking, the Fourth Commandment, and the Suppression of Authentic Feelings

Interview, June 2005

You have established that the Fourth Commandment ("Thou shalt honor thy father and thy mother") is detrimental to the healthy emotional life of a child. This will come as quite a shock for many people. How did you discover that the only function of this "honorable injunction" is in fact manipulation and subordination of the child?

The commandment is not detrimental to the child but later to the adult. All children love their parents, and they wouldn't need a commandment to tell them to do so. But when we become adults and realize that our love was exploited and we were abused, we should be able to experience our true feelings, including rage, and not be forced to honor parents who were cruel to us. Most people are afraid of their "negative" feelings toward their parents, so they take them out on their children and in this way perpetuate the cycle of violence. It is here that I see the destructive effect of the Fourth Commandment. Since there is as yet no commandment or law that would inhibit parents from dumping their pent-up anger on their offspring, even the most violent behavior displayed by parents can still be called "upbringing."

You even go so far as to assert that the Fourth Commandment causes physical ailments. How would you explain this link?

It is the suppression of authentic emotions and feelings that makes us ill. The reason why we suppress our genuine feelings is fear. The child's unconscious fear of violent parents can stay with us all our lives if we refuse to confront it by remaining in a state of denial.

We take it for granted that parents "love" their children. Unfortunately, this is more often than not a myth. Is love, seasoned with "only" occasional "educational" spanking, possible?

As parents, we should know that violent upbringing, in whatever form and however well intended, will kill love.

Why is spanking always wrong?

Spanking is always an abuse of power. It is humiliating and it creates fear. A state of fear can only teach children to be distrustful and hide their true feelings. In addition, they learn from their parents that violence is the right way of resolving conflicts, and that they themselves are bad or unworthy and thus deserve correction. These children will soon forget why they were spanked. They will submit very quickly, but later in life they will do the same to weaker persons. By spanking we teach violence. Children's bodies have learned the lesson of violence from their parents over a long period, and we cannot expect them to suddenly forget these lessons when they have religious values preached at them, which their bodies do not understand anyway. Instead, their bodies retain the memory of being spanked.

Many despicable acts are committed in the name of parental love. How would you define real parental love?

I love my children if I can respect them with all their feelings and their needs and try to fulfill those needs as best I can. If I see them not as persons whose rights are just as sacrosanct as my own, but as objects that I have to correct, then that is not love.

You speak of child abuse in our culture as a forbidden issue. Why is this so? What is needed to change this state of affairs?

The issue is forbidden because most of us were spanked in child-hood, and we don't want to be reminded of that. We learned as children that spanking is harmless. We had to learn this lie in order to survive. Now, as adults, we don't want to know the truth, that in fact spanking is harmful. It is interesting that people react aggressively when you say "Don't spank your child." They become even more aggressive if you say "You were spanked yourself and suffered as a child; you were forced to deny your pain in order to survive." They would rather kill themselves than admit the truth and feel the pain of having been humiliated and deprived of love when they were spanked by someone five times bigger than them-selves. These aggressive reactions are understandable. Imagine how you would feel if you went out on the street and somebody five times bigger than you suddenly laid into you and you didn't even understand why. Children cannot bear this truth; they have no choice but to repress it. But adults can face up to it. As adults, we are not so alone. We can look for witnesses, and we have an awareness we didn't have when we were children.

You say that hatred is better than the adoration of abusive parents, because it is a sign of our vitality. With regard to their parents many people find themselves trapped in a chain of self-deception; they idealize them. How can we direct hatred, rage, and anger at the proper recipient (and not at ourselves or our partners)?

We can try to become emotionally honest with ourselves and find the courage to confront the reality of our childhood. Unfortunately, there are not many people who really want to know what happened in the first years of their lives. But their number seems to be growing. Some years ago we created forums in different languages on the Internet. This proved helpful for many people. Adults who were abused as children and who want to know more precisely what happened to them, and how they actually feel about it, can share their memories with other survivors in a safe environment and gradually get in touch with their true histories. Thanks to the empathy of feeling witnesses, they achieve greater emotional clarity that helps them to change the way they treat their children. Of course, they also become more honest with their partners and themselves once they achieve a clearer understanding of the causes of those strong emotions they have been repressing.

One of the fundamental psychological truths is that persons emotionally deprived in childhood will hope all their lives to receive the love denied to them. Why is it so hard to accept that we weren't important to anyone? Many even prefer to commit suicide instead.

Yes, you are quite right. Some prefer to commit suicide or willingly accept a chronic illness. Others prefer to demonstrate what they learned as children (violence, cruelty, perversion) by becoming dictators or serial killers rather than acknowledge their early deprivation. The more deprived and mistreated people were in their childhood, the more they stay attached to their parents, waiting for them to change. They also seem to remain bogged down in their childhood fear. This fear in the mind of a tormented child makes any kind of rebellion unthinkable, even if the parents are already dead.

While we are on the subject, Slovenia is famous for its high percentage of suicides. How would you tackle this problem?

Like depression, suicide is always the consequence of denied suffering in childhood. I have written an article about depression (see chapter 1, "Depression: Compulsive Self-Deception," in this volume). There I refer to many examples of very successful stars, such as Dalida, the famous Egyptian singer, who achieved everything they desired and were admired and famous. But later in life they succumbed to depression, and many of them committed suicide. In all these cases it was not the present that made them suffer. It was the denied traumas of their childhood that made them feel miserable because they were never consciously acknowledged. The body was left alone with its knowledge.

How do you think morality and ethics come about? Why does someone become moral or immoral?

Never by preaching, only by experience. No one is born wicked. It is ridiculous to think, as people did in the Middle Ages, that Satan can foist a wicked child onto a family, and that the only way of making it into a decent person is by beating the daylights out of it. A tormented child will become a tormentor and will certainly turn into a cruel parent unless in childhood he or she was lucky enough to encounter a "helping witness," a person with whom the child could feel safe, loved, protected, and respected. Experiences of this kind teach us what love can be. Then such a child will not become a tyrant but will be able to respect other people and have empathy for them. It is very significant that, in the childhood of all dictators I have examined, I didn't find evidence of one single "helping witness." The child thus had no choice but to glorify the violence it had endured.

Religious education teaches us to forgive our tormentors. Should we really forgive them? Is it in fact possible to do so?

It is understandable that we should want to forgive and forget and not feel the pain. But this never works in the long run. It turns out sooner or later that this path will not get us anywhere. Take the many instances of sexual abuse committed by representatives of the church. They have forgiven their parents for sexual abuse or other abuses of their power. But what are many of them doing? They are repeating the "sins" of their parents precisely *because* they have forgiven them. If they were able to consciously condemn the deeds of their parents, they wouldn't feel urged to emulate them and to molest and confuse children by forcing them to stay silent, quite as if this were the most normal thing in the world and not a crime. This is simply self-delusion. Religions can have an enormous power over our minds and force us into many kinds of self-deception. But they have not the slightest influence on our bodies, which know our true emotions perfectly well and insist that we respect them.

Is compassion for Milošević or Saddam Hussein acceptable?

I have always had compassion for children but never for an adult tyrant. Here, I have sometimes been misunderstood, especially in my description of the childhood of Adolf Hitler. Some readers didn't understand how I could feel compassion for the young Adolf but never for the adult Hitler, who became a monster exactly because he denied the suffering caused him by the severe humiliations inflicted on him by his father. As a child, Adolf Hitler was of course unable to defend his dignity. But he also remained submissive in adulthood. He feared and honored his father his whole life, suffered from attacks of panic at night, and his immense hatred was directed at all Jews and half-Jews.

The fiercest champions of their parents are those who suffered the worst emotional deprivation at their hands. There is a very cruel mechanism at work here, and it produces a very pessimistic vision of life. Is there hope for those so badly wounded in this way?

I don't think that my view is pessimistic. On the contrary, I believe that if we can understand how the cycle of violence functions, we can share our knowledge with others and cooperate in putting a stop to it. But if we believe that people are born with genes that make them violent, we cannot change anything. Although this opinion *is* highly pessimistic, and untenable into the bargain, many so-called intelligent individuals share it, preferring to believe in genetic causes rather than see how their parents treated them and feel the pain. But by feeling the pain they could liberate themselves from the compulsion to repeat the misdeeds behind it and thus become responsible adults. This statement is by no means pessimistic.

Is there any hope for those who don't find a witness?

An informative book can also function as a kind of witness. The more we speak and write about this problem, the more witnesses will be available in the world, well-informed witnesses who can help children to feel respected and safe and help adults to bear their truth. Denial not only urges us to repeat, it also consumes a great deal of energy. Illnesses, eating disorders, and substance addictions are the consequences.

"Positive thinking" is just as harmful as religious injunctions to forgive, turn the other cheek, and love those who hate us. Should we shun New Age self-help manuals?

Yes, you are right. "Positive thinking" is no remedy at all. It is a form of self-deception, a flight from the truth. It cannot help because the body knows better. In my article "What Is Hatred?" (see chapter 4 in this volume) I go into greater detail on this point.

What are the political consequences of your writing?

The political consequences of my writing are not yet widely understood. People love to see human cruelty as a mystery and to consider it innate. Also, some ideologies are good at camouflaging the actual reasons for cruelty. Look what happened in Yugoslavia when Serbian soldiers were allowed to take revenge for the denied pain of children beaten in their early years. Milošević gave them the permission to do so, and this was enough. There was no need for any instructions to be cruel; the soldiers had them stored in their bodies. For years they had been exposed to cruelty as children and were never allowed to react. Now they could take revenge on innocent people in the conviction that they were fighting for an ethnic cause. Likewise, millions of Germans who were beaten into submission as children became sadistic and perverted adults as soon as they were allowed by Hitler's regime to act in this way.

Many years ago, in my book *For Your Own Good*, I described the upbringing inflicted on all those Germans who later fell in with Hitler's crazed ideas. At that time people thought it necessary to beat children as soon as possible, immediately after birth, so that they would become "decent" people. Now, thanks to increasing research on the child brain, we know that the structure of the brain is dependent on experience. We all come into this world with a brain that is not yet fully structured. It takes at least the first three years to complete this process. The structure of the brain is conditioned by early experience (whether a child is loved or maltreated). So it is no surprise that in countries where beating small children is permitted and has become normal practice, wars and even genocide and terrorism seem inevitable. For that reason we need laws prohibiting corporal punishment for children. Unfortunately, such laws only exist in a number of smaller countries, while bigger ones, like the United States, are a long way from even contemplating such legislation. There, physical correction for children at school is permitted in as many as twenty-two states.*

From the http://nospank.net Web site you can learn that spanking at home and paddling in schools are still felt to be absolutely normal by most Americans. They were spanked and paddled when they were small, and now they insist on their *right* to treat their children the same way. There is hope, however, that this important Web site and others like it will bring about a change sooner or later. The links between so-called "educational" violence and atrocities in "political" life have become so obvious to some people that they cannot be passed over in silence forever. One day, everyone will

---

* Corporal punishment is currently legal in twenty-one U.S. states.

know that human cruelty is not innate, that it is produced and learned in childhood.

The *First* Commandment should be: "Honor your children so they won't need to set up protective barriers against old pain and defend themselves against phantom enemies with terrible weapons capable of destroying the world."

What is wrong with current psychoanalytic practice? Why were you "expelled" from the Psychoanalytic Association?

I was not expelled from the Psychoanalytic Association; I merely challenged their traditional way of thinking and their denial of childhood suffering. I eventually had to admit that psychoanalysis is no exception in this respect. The way in which Freud used the story of Oedipus is very significant. It shows very clearly the blame put on the child and the tendency to protect the parents. Freud seems to have forgotten that Oedipus was first a victim of his parents and was pushed by them into the role of a "sinner." His parents sent him away as a very small child. It is highly enlightening to read the true story of Oedipus.

As for current psychoanalytic practice, I believe that it safeguards the protection of parents by adhering to a variety of rules such as neutrality (instead of partiality for the child victim) and by focusing on fantasies (instead of confrontation with the reality of cruel upbringing).

You describe the emotional life of quite a few of the most highly regarded writers of the modern age. Who would you cite as someone who has successfully overcome the traumatic conflict with his or her parents?

This is a very interesting question that nobody has asked me before. I have been looking around for a long time, but I cannot find even one well-known writer who doesn't believe that we must eventually forgive our parents. Even if they see the cruelty of their upbringing, they feel guilty about seeing it. Franz Kafka was one of the bravest writers on this subject, but at that time nobody could endorse his knowledge. So he felt guilty and died as a very young man, like Proust, Rimbaud, Schiller, Chekhov, Nietzsche, and so many others who began to grasp the truth but were scared of it. Why is it so difficult to bear the truth of having been abused in childhood? Why do we prefer to blame ourselves? Because blaming ourselves protects us from the pain. I think that the worst pain we have to go through in order to become emotionally honest is to admit that we were never loved when we needed it most. It is easy to say this, but it is very, very hard to feel it. And to accept it, to root out the expectation that one day my parents will change and love me. But unlike children, adults can rid themselves of this illusion, for the benefit of their health and their offspring. People who absolutely want to know their truth are capable of doing just that. And I believe that these individuals will change the world. They will not be "heroes"; they may be quite unassuming people, but there is no doubt that their emotional honesty will at some point be able to break down the wall of ignorance, denial, and violence. The pain of not being loved is only a feeling; a feeling is never destructive when it is directed at the person who caused the pain involved in it. Then even hatred is not destructive, as long as it is conscious and not acted out. But it can be very destructive, indeed highly dangerous for oneself and others, if it is denied and directed at scapegoats.

19

Combating Denial

Interview, July 2005

Fairy tales and myths can tell us a great deal about our culture and our perception of the world. One of the best-known fairy tales that small children are sooner or later confronted with is "Little Red Riding Hood." Among thousands of other folk tales this particular one stands out as incredibly popular. What does it tell us about our attitude to children in our culture?

It tells us that it is quite normal practice to sacrifice children and make them the victims of parental attitudes. The mother sends the child to her grandmother all on her own and cares nothing for the dangers lurking in the forest (the wolf).

I am always shocked by the "official" interpretation that the mother of Little Red Riding Hood is well intentioned and caring. She sends her young daughter into a dangerous forest explaining that this is an "honorable" task (poor grandmother is sick after all). I find this mother cruel, wicked, perverted even. Would you agree?

Yes, I agree, because she must have known that there are wolves in the forest. After all, she tells her daughter not to stray from the path. However, she doesn't prepare the child for the dangers lurking there, she denies them. As a result, the child trusts the wolf, tells him where her grandmother lives, and even when she later sees the wolf in Grandma's bed, she talks to him as if he were Grandma. She has already adopted her mother's denial. She shares her blindness and becomes the naïve victim of the wolf, perhaps symbolizing the incestuous father to whom mothers often deliver their daughters. They protect their own fathers by suppressing the memories of being abused in their childhood and *for this very reason* are blind to the dangers their daughters are in.

Whenever I addressed some of the nastier aspects of my childhood, my attempts were rejected, and I was told that everything has its good and its bad sides, so we should look on the bright side of life and adopt a positive attitude. In such argumentation even abuse has something to be said for it. How would you react to this kind of relativism?

This kind of thinking is almost necessary in childhood; it is a survival strategy. Even if they have incredibly brutal parents, children do not want to die, so they absolutely have to believe that what they are enduring is not the whole truth. And of course there are moments when the brutal father seems to change. He takes you out fishing, and you can then feel loved for a while. If he later uses you as a toy or as an object of his sexual desires, you can escape your fears because you still have the good memory of the fishing outing or other such occasions. In this way we survive our childhood, and most people try to live only with these good memories by suppressing the bad ones. In so doing they are supported by religions and almost all philosophies known to me. But I think that as adults we have the ability to take the facts seriously and to know that we are no longer in mortal danger if we do so. We can make the effort to see that, for whatever reasons, our parents cannot have loved us if they were able to victimize us so many times, without caring for our feelings, our pain, and our future. This awareness helps us to get rid of our self-destructive feelings of guilt. By condemning our parents' deeds we become free from the compulsion to repeat such acts with our own children.

How would you define abuse?

Abuse means to me using a person for whatever I want them for, without asking for their consent, without respecting their will and their interests. With children, it is very easy to do so because they are loving, they trust their parents and most adults, and they don't realize that they have been abused, that their love has been exploited. Especially if they were forced to ignore their emotions from the outset, they may have lost all sensitivity for the alarm signals. A small girl will follow a neighbor who promises her chocolate down into his cellar, although she may feel uncomfortable about it. But if she has learned from the beginning of her life that her feelings don't matter and that she should obey adults even if she doesn't like the idea, then she will go along with that neighbor. She will behave like Little Red Riding Hood in the fairy tale. And she may later suffer in her relations with men for her whole life, if she doesn't come to terms actively with that early experience in the cellar. However, if she does, she will no longer be in danger of becoming a victim of rape or any other kind of molestation.

How many people do you think have been abused in childhood?

It is harder to estimate how many people were *not* abused. I do know people who were not exploited in their childhood, who were loved, cared for, and allowed to live in accordance with their true feelings. I saw them as babies, and I now see that they are able to give their children the same respect they got from their parents. But I don't know many like that. Spanking children is still regarded as harmless and beneficial all over the world. I think that about 90 percent of the world population has been abused in this way more or less severely. Every day on TV you can see what the most severely abused are doing now that they have become adults who deny their suffering and admire and respect their abusive parents. There's a simple test for this. You just go around the world asking the most cruel people what their parents were like. The answer you get from the worst tyrants will often be: My parents were wonderful people. They wanted the best for me, but I was an obstinate brat.

Human blindness to abuse can be astonishing. Even when confronted with their own obvious abuse, people still believe in the myth of being loved and keep abusing their children (and other people's). How would you most effectively "open their eyes" to what they are doing? Is this possible at all?

I can't open the eyes of others. They will quickly close them again. They don't want to see—or they are afraid to see—the truth because they expect to be punished by their parents, or by God, who represents them. I can only open my own eyes and say what I am seeing. And sometimes people feel encouraged to open one eye or even both. They are then surprised that no punishment is visited on them, that they feel even relief since they have stopped betraying themselves.

People normally prefer to deny that they have been abused. Would
you interpret eating disorders, obsession with diets, nail-biting, "inof-
fensive social drinking," thinking about suicide, asthma, taking drugs,
or even the self-destructive "need" for unhealthy junk food or ciga-
rettes as unambiguous evidence of emotional or physical abuse?

Yes, absolutely. All these illnesses or addictions are screams emitted by a body trying to make itself heard. Instead of listening and
trying to understand these screams, many have chosen headlong
flight.

You say the body is wise and can't be fooled. The good news is that if
we listen to it, we can be cured of physical symptoms. But if we are
too busy denying its needs and its memories, we condemn ourselves
to living in an invisible hell. Everything is perfect, but we are cut off
from our true emotions and destined to live a hollow, superficial life,
and our body becomes our enemy. How can we become friends with
our body, which frequently harbors such unpleasant truths?

First, we have to stop avoiding the truth. Once we have lived
through one or more experiences of this kind, we will realize that
the truth didn't kill us, that in fact it made us feel better eventually.
If you decide not to take your pills when you get a headache and
try to find out instead when exactly the headache started, what
happened just before, you might be lucky enough to understand
why your body needed a headache just now, what happened today
that would make you feel miserable if you gave your full attention to the event. Once you do that, a very painful emotion may
arise that demands to be felt. However, after this feeling is over, a
solution to your plight may appear. But in any case, to your great
surprise, you realize that your headache has disappeared without

any medication. If you have already experienced such spontaneous disappearance of a symptom, nobody will ever be able to convince you that your headache absolutely needs aspirin to make it go away. The drug prevents you from understanding yourself. But this understanding may be essential for your health.

The distinction between feelings and emotions is fundamental to understanding the mechanism of denial. Why is it so important to know the difference?

If you no longer try to deny your past, you are freer to trust your emotions. They convey your history to you, often unconsciously and often through the messages of your body. Your mind can learn to understand these messages and in this way to transform the emotions into conscious feelings. If you know your feelings, you have the best protection you can have. If you fight them, you will feel constantly imperiled, afraid of things that happened decades ago and are no longer real dangers.

A child must repress the experience of abuse in order to survive. How does such a life-enhancing mechanism transform itself into a life-stifling one?

This mechanism doesn't transform itself. It remains the same, but later does not adapt to new circumstances. We don't need it as adults, so we must let it go. Otherwise we can't take advantage of being adult. We continue to live as dependent children. If you take a trip on a plane, you need to fasten your seat belt for your own safety. But after leaving the plane, back down on the ground, you no longer need it. No one in their right mind would leave it on. But most people do exactly that. They walk around on earth still wearing what was a lifesaver for them in the air. They adhere as adults to the denial that saved their lives in childhood. And what was necessary *then* becomes life-stifling now.

You use the term "poisonous pedagogy." I understand it as an authoritarian form of education. Does permissive education have similar effects?

In the English editions of my books the notion of "*Schwarze Pädagogik*" has been translated as "poisonous pedagogy." In *For Your Own Good*, I describe how these methods for producing obedient, submissive children kill their natural capacity for empathy. The permissive education of the post-1968 era was harmful in other ways, but perhaps it was less destructive. It often meant total neglect of the children's need for protection and communication. And it was also a kind of exploitation of children's love for the sake of an adult ideology. This very often led to severe sexual abuse, concealed by Freud's theory of infantile sexuality, and to deep confusion in the child's sense of identity. But I don't think that permissive education was as brutal as the authoritarian variety, which eventually led to millions of people willingly following Adolf Hitler as his obedient servants and henchmen.

When I was asked to prepare a short summary of your book, I wrote that you discuss the abuse of gifted children. Then I was told that I should avoid the term "abuse" because it is too offensive, brutal, and revolting. Instead, I was forced to say that you deal with parents' "lack of understanding" and "disregard" for their children. What's your comment on this?

It is very common to be accused of being offensive if you "call a spade a spade" instead of resorting to euphemisms. It is customary practice everywhere to hush up the brutality of parents and vilify the people who denounce this kind of "upbringing." Since this is the way we have learned to behave, we don't dare to relinquish it, and we are quickly intimidated.

You write: "Traumata stored in the brain but denied by our conscious minds will always be visited on the next generation." Can you say a little more about this mechanism? Is an infant bound to be deprived of its innocence simply because it was born to parents who deny traumata?

Yes. Unfortunately, miracles are very rare. If parents say "Spanking never did me any harm," they will do the same to their children without a second thought. But if they can see that their parents' treatment mutilated their lives, they will do their best to spare their children the same fate. They will go in search of information, and they will not want to remain captives to denial and ignorance.

I notice that a lot of people react allergically when they see a truly childlike child unburdened by guilt and abuse. They just can't stand it. They go on saying that children must be socialized as quickly as possible, in other words taken away from their parents and put into nursery school so that they can learn to "adjust." They preach the blessings of socialization as if it were a supremely sacred and noble cause. I find that this exerts enormous social pressure. In this context socialization frequently means nothing other than adjustment to cruelty. Why is a child who is alive, genuine, and pure unbearable or even sinful in their eyes? Why must children like that be mutilated so that they will resemble them?

Because in the parents, or other adults, the child's creativity and vitality can trigger the repressed pain of having been stifled in their own childhood. They are afraid of feeling the pain, so they do whatever they can to defuse the triggers. By insisting on obedience they kill children's vitality, they victimize them as they themselves were victimized before. Most parents don't want to hurt their children; they do it automatically, by repeating what they themselves learned when they were small. We can help them to refrain from this destructive behavior by explaining to them why it is so destructive. Then they can wake up and make a choice.

V

FROM THE DIARY OF A MOTHER

20

From the Diary
of a Mother

1

Today, I have something to celebrate! I haven't seen her for months. She said she didn't want to come, she needed space between herself and her mother. In therapy she was reexperiencing her childhood, the feelings she had when she was small. That was why she didn't want to see me. But she still calls me from time to time. When she does, it always seems to me as if she is testing whether her feelings are telling her the truth, whether I really am the omnipotent mother who exploits and dominates her, only to abandon her again, someone she cannot empathize with, someone who always has to be in the right and hurts her constantly without her being able to defend herself. On the phone we chat first about inconsequential things. I feel pretty sure of myself because I know that I have developed over the last thirty years. No longer am I that uncertain young woman who dumped all her fears and anxieties on her firstborn child. I know that today I can love my daughter as she is, as long as I perceive her as my child and not as my own demanding mother. That is a mistake I still sometimes make, though less often than I used to. But those phone calls are still a problem. However relaxed we are at the beginning, sooner or later we relapse into our old roles.

It was different before she started going for therapy. For many years we had a trusting relationship, and we could really talk to each other. But things have changed. Now she frequently experiences herself as a little child, which means that my role is cut out for me. There's no escape. Whatever I do is wrong. If I'm not at home when she calls, then I'm the absent, neglectful mother she cannot make contact with. If I'm there, all friendly and interested, she holds that against me because it doesn't square with her feelings. Those feelings tell her the story of quite a different mother. So she gets annoyed because my behavior doesn't confirm her feelings. But when I sense this annoyance, I am tempted to try and help her by adjusting. I know what I did to her when she was small, and I'm trying to make up for it. I want to say to her: "You're right. Everything your feelings suggest to you is true. I repeatedly left you on your own without realizing what that must be like for a baby. I exerted my power without suspecting what I was doing to you. Now I can feel how painful that is. Now you too can feel and discover your childhood reality. It would be almost uncanny if you were not to do that. But it hurts me so much when you are cold and unapproachable. I don't deserve that kind of treatment anymore, and I need contact with you very badly. But your rejection and my abandonment tell me how you experienced yourself as a child: as someone I had abandoned. You were always kind and loving to me, you listened, I could bare my heart to you, you were understanding, you helped me. And now here we are, confronted with the truth about those years, a truth that is so dreadfully painful."

This is why I am so apprehensive about your coming to see me after all this time. Two months ago you called me from somewhere a long way away and told me things you can never say when we're in the same room together. It really hurt. First, I thought you were being unjust, but when I tried to see it all with your eyes, I realized that you are right. But initially I experienced your accusations in the situation of the little girl I once was, a little girl who had no chance of doing the right thing because the accusations leveled at her had quite simply to do with the fact that she was there at all. Whatever she did was wrong. I experienced you as if you were my mother, who rejected me when I was born, who didn't want me. All my life I tried in vain to win her favor, and finally she made me into a caring mother so that she could remain a child. I experienced you as if you were my father, who sought in me the warmth and tenderness his wife was unable to give him, but in a way that I was completely unable to deal with. I felt inadequate to the demands of both my parents, and finally I embarked on an unending and superhuman effort to live up to their expectations without defending myself. You were the only one whose expectations I defended myself against, but you were only a little baby. At the time, I was unable to see how absurd it was. Now I have realized, and I feel that if you were a baby today, I could be different with you. But you are an adult woman, and every time we meet, you confront me with your own history. That makes me feel the same way as I felt with my parents—forced into a vicarious role, never allowed to be the person I really was, always being made into something they needed me to be, so that they invariably communicated with the role they had imposed on me but never with me.

———————

I AM SITTING here writing this down because I don't want our first meeting after all this time to be burdened by my past. I shall keep my feelings to myself instead of delegating them to you, the way I did in your childhood. But as I do so, I see once again how I was forced to close myself off as a child. There was no one I could expect to understand my feelings, so I said nothing in an attempt to make it easier for the others. I tried my best to understand them, and by doing so I was in danger of losing myself.

I BROKE OFF when the doorbell rang. We sat together for five hours, and it was entirely different from what I had anticipated. The panic fear I felt before you arrived disappeared completely once you were actually here. You were genuine, vibrant, direct. Your criticisms were a relief because they put things in a clear perspective again. You are beginning to realize the sheer weight I placed on you. It still rests on your shoulders, and you are doing everything you can to free yourself of that ballast. For the first time in your life you are impervious to my pain, and I fluctuate between imploring you to have mercy on me and the certainty that you are on the right road, that the slightest compromise might cause you to feel like a worm trapped beneath the crushing weight of a huge building. All I can do now is to accept the fact that you are living your own life without knowing whether we will ever be able to talk to each other the way we used to. Maybe it will never happen again. Maybe I will have to do without your help. I try to imagine how you experience me, the burden I represent for you, a burden you want to cast off, the burden of my knowledge and experience that leave you too little scope to go out and experience things for yourself. Not only that, but also my own distress, the life I missed out on and expected you to substitute for, my failed marriage I wanted you to compensate for by choosing the right partner, the fears I disguised as concern for your well-being, crippling your self-confidence and expecting gratitude in return. For the first time you have told me that my concern for you makes you anxious, inhibits your decisions. You have the feeling that you are always account-able to me for the decisions you make because I want the best for you and know everything so much better than you do.

ANYONE WHO KNOWS me would tell you that this is all in your imagination, that you have a tolerant mother who supports you in your decisions, who lets you live your own life and is glad that you are so independent. That's how others see it, and we both thought the same way until recently. But now you are finding out how it really was, and when you tell me what you are discovering, I see that it is true because at the same time I understand—perhaps also for the first time—how my mother restricted me with her anxiety and how I unconsciously passed that on to you in a differ-ent and very subtle way without realizing what I was doing. My mother discouraged me from all the physical activities I enjoyed, including sports, and she succeeded brilliantly by warning me of the disasters and accidents that might so easily happen. As a child, I actually confirmed her warnings by suffering a number of accidents, which taught me how justified those warnings had been. But she never warned me about trying to do well at school because there she wanted me to achieve everything that she had never achieved herself. After what you told me today, I have the impression that I haven't moved as far away from my mother as I would have liked to. In that respect our conversation has helped me a lot. Suddenly, I see my mother much more clearly, and there were lots of other things I'd have liked to ask you. But at the same time, I appreciate that it is for you to decide how far you want to go. You want to decide when you want to see me, you need distance. You are on your way into a new world of independence, and when we talk on the phone you don't want to put yourself in the position of asking questions, currying approval, making requests, and letting me make you feel uncertain again. I must respect that, even though it hurts. Perhaps, deep down, I do not really need you in actual terms. For the first time I am beginning to feel my own need in your presence. Earlier, I used to deny my distress. I thought that when I called you I did so for your sake, that I was prompted to do so by my love and concern for you, because you needed my help and sympathy. How deceptive love and the best intentions can be in reality! But there's nothing I can do about it. All I can do is to try not to be evasive when my children talk to me. If that succeeds, then almost automatically it lessens the temptation to pretend, both to ourselves and to others. Trying to force a child to be grateful in return for a show of love that merely conceals anxiety and need is anything but honest. It is a game we have all played. When we were children, this dross was sold to us as pure gold. We would do anything to get it; we called it parental love and thought our whole lives would be insufficient to pay it back. The other side of the mask was never revealed because we never dared to say no. It only becomes apparent when those inauthentic feelings fail to make an effect. This is something I have understood again, but in a new and different way, after our conversation today.

YOU SAY: "I don't want your concern, even if it's well meant. I don't want your help, even if, on the face of it, I could do with it. I want to help myself or ask others for help." When you talk to me like this, I should be glad, even if my behavior had always been sincerely meant. But I stand there with my arms hanging by my sides, feeling rejected, good-for-nothing, abandoned. This makes me realize that I have often deceived you. What I called help and concern for you was in fact the need to make myself indispensable and to attach you to me. And now you have gone away, you no longer need me as you used to, and I feel abandoned like a child that has tried to give her parents everything they need but realizes that her attempts were not good enough, that all the effort in the world will never get her the love she needs. Your refusal to go on playing this game has made me aware of the disguises involved. They conceal the helplessness, and behind the pretense of total devotion to the child there is nothing but the desire to perpetuate her attachment with the manacles of self-blame and eternal gratitude.

2

It is very late, Nina. You have been to see me again, and I have just read through what I wrote not so long ago. As I do so, I realize how much easier it is to do without the presence of an adult child once we achieve a degree of inner distance and rely on analysis, as I did at the beginning. I am struck by the fact that I started out by writing about you in the third person. I cannot do this any longer; from now on I shall speak to you directly. I feel that you are so close that I should like to hug you as I used to. I hear myself saying "Now everything's fine, isn't it? You'll be coming for Christmas with your husband." I sense the fact that he hates me, but in his case I know exactly that I am not to blame for that hatred, in fact that I am not really the target of it. But I will go to any lengths; I will be nice to him and make sure that Christmas is enjoyable for all of us. Perhaps Gisela and Robert will come too, and then we'll be a proper family again. But at the word "family" I find myself tensing up. "Family"; "We'll be nice to each other"; "We'll let bygones be bygones." All these words stir up old and painful memories. My whole body rebels at the idea of sweeping feelings under the carpet on which the lovely Christmas tree stands, singing cheerful carols, swallowing the tears, and thinking all the time: Just this one evening, let it be a success, don't spoil it for the others and yourself, you can cry tomorrow. No. I refuse. The lies and compromises are suffocating me. If I hugged you now, it would be a sincere and heartfelt hug. But this gesture might be a new prison for you. For the moment, you might be glad, it would satisfy your old longings for an embrace, or perhaps compassion for me would stop you from thrusting my arms away. That compassion would also be sincere, but the whole thing would be an abuse of my old power, a seduction of the child, my adult daughter, who had to bite back her accusations for thirty years and now has to let them out. I would be ignoring your own truth, and that is not love. I feel the need to embrace you, to seek you out, to knock at your door, fling my arms around your neck. And I know you would be kind to me. I could cry in your arms, and you would console me. I know you are the one person who is not indifferent to my tears. I could get all this from you because I was once the most important person in your life, in anyone's life—your mother. It would be so lovely to enjoy that, to warm myself in the presence of my grown-up, intelligent, warmhearted daughter and borrow her strength, if only for a few hours—to obtain from you what neither Gisela nor Robert ever had to give me because they could be my children and I never made them into my own mother as I did with you, my eldest daughter. And that is why I shall *not* go and knock on your door. It would be a betrayal. I would drive you back into the role of a mother, a role you are quite right to reject.

I would rekindle your illusions, the longing for an unselfish mother, at a time when you are liberating yourself of those deep-seated illusions and starting to see the truth. I wrote that last sentence instinctively, but reading it again I realize that it contains a lie. What an easy time lies always have! They get in everywhere. That is why it was so hard for me to detect the untruth in that sentence. I say that the reason why I shall not visit you is to avoid arousing illusions in you. Once again I am claiming that I have made this decision for your sake. But it might be that I am not thinking on your behalf, that I might go all the same because I just want to see you. The risk I would be running is that you might not welcome me by slipping into the role of the concerned mother-daughter, as you used to. Instead, you might be annoyed and discouraging. Then I would experience my pain, the humiliation, the rejection. If I am truly honest with myself, it is this that I want to avoid. I don't want to impose myself; I need to be sure that you really want me there. Now I realize how easily mothers can think themselves wanted because a little child cannot do without them. I find it shameful that we mothers can exploit this fact all our lives and that many women never realize how shameful it is.

FACING UP TO reality is not easy. But would I find it easier to celebrate Christmas in a hypocritical way? No, I would not. So I have made a choice. I intend to look the truth in the face, cost what it may. It is the only alternative. I can no longer flee from suffering. I know that this is no great sacrifice because celebrating Christmas under false pretenses also made me suffer, though that feeling was elusive and inarticulate. So this is not a moral decision;

it is an option for the lesser of two evils. The biggest evil in my life has always been situations where I was forced to restrain myself and pass things over in silence.

Why Christmas, you may ask? What do I have against celebrating something that means so much to everyone? Do I want to deny them their joy? Am I jealous because I can never feel that joy, because I have always resisted being expected to enjoy decorating the house, baking cookies, and giving people presents just because the official time has come to do so? For me joy is something spontaneous that cannot be planned beforehand, and my creativity deserts me when I have to make cookies and decorate the table to welcome my mother-in-law, who cannot stand the sight of me. I cannot be kind and cheerful to order, I never have any bright ideas for gifts that I *have to* come up with. I take no pleasure in gifts I do not need, so I tend to think that it must be the same for others as well. I have trouble giving someone a present if I cannot be sure that it really is something they need. If I give someone something that takes no account of their needs, I fear that I have offended them, whether they are aware of it or not.

Did I feel differently when I was a child? Then I could look forward to the presents and the candles, enjoy my parents' beautiful clothes and happy faces, relish the exceptional situation, because so many things were important on this one day that conflict and trouble were out of the question. But were they really? My father did not come home drunk; my mother spared him open criticism. But on many occasions I felt the tension that hung over Christmas dinner, I read the mute reproach in the eyes of my mother, who had spared no effort for our sake—or that of the baby Jesus—who presided over the exquisite meal looking as if she might collapse from exhaustion at any moment even though the servants had done most of the work. If she really had to suppress all the feelings that assail me on such occasions today, then it must have cost her so much effort that she really was exhausted. My father played the loving daddy, the relaxed, warmhearted, goodly man exhibiting a childlike pleasure in the glow of the candles and the wonderful food and enjoying the beautiful, harmonious atmosphere to the utmost. Forgotten were the blows he had inflicted on his children the day before, the harsh words with which he had silenced his wife. We sang "Silent Night" and "God Rest Ye Merry, Gentlemen," and there was the devil to pay if everyone around him was not silent and merry. His wife's exhausted features tensed him up in a way that we children were quicker to notice than he was. We sensed the storm that was brewing and tried to stave it off with our carols, often successfully. My mother did her best; we all did our best—no one wanted to hear the sound of a door slamming. My father's good mood was a precious boon that must not be set at risk.

In most cases we children passed the test. But there were exceptions. If one of us could no longer stand the unspoken tension between my parents and said something provocative or started acting out of line, this violation of the rules was immediately punished. Feelings ran high, and the children had to look on in silence as my parents hurled their accusations at one another, my mother complaining of her exhaustion, my father of the money the Christmas presents had cost him, of all the work he had to do, all the meetings that went on into the night: "And it's all for you!" "Including the pub?" my mother asked, unerringly seeking out his most sensitive spot to strike at. Alcohol, his only refuge, was under attack; his guilt feelings were aroused; he hit back. We children were sent to bed; Christmas was over. We lay there in the dark, thinking it wouldn't be so bad if this were an ordinary day. It would have been normal and predictable, the same old thing over again. But on this night we were not prepared for it; we were defenseless. We had really believed that this was the night when the baby Jesus and the angels would watch over us and ensure that none of the things would happen that we had to go through every other day.

I REALIZE NOW how these experiences have conditioned my deep-seated dislike of Christmas. I didn't want to be reminded of it, but on every occasion I sensed my mother's fatigue, the fear of my father's bad temper if things did not go according to plan, the children's efforts to make sure that things stayed peaceful, and the sadness those efforts caused me. I felt the artificiality of the situation to be much stronger than it actually was. I felt nasty and guilty because it was Christmas and my feelings were not in tune with the message of peace and goodwill it proclaimed. I despaired to hear people I believed to be experienced preaching the necessity of combating the hatred within us so that love and charity could take possession of our hearts. How did other people manage to do that? Why couldn't I? Why did my anger at my husband come to a climax at Christmas, a celebration I experienced as a ritual, as a compulsion to insincerity, an abuse of my true feelings, an occasion for blackmailing the children into gratitude and good behavior with the help of expensive presents? How do other people pull it off, I asked myself throughout my marriage to Karl. How can they be joyful on demand?

PERHAPS THINGS ARE completely different for other people. Perhaps they never experienced tension between their parents at

Christmas, perhaps they have only fond and loving memories of that season. But for me the story of the Nativity always had a darker side: the menacing tyranny of Herod, the family without a roof over their heads, the indifference of other people. Herod always reminds me of how easy it is to pronounce a judgment on the child within us, how implicitly we can rely on the world to help us execute that judgment, how lonely society makes us if we try to save the innocent, helpless child within. Mary and Joseph found refuge in Egypt. Today there is nowhere we can escape to. Contempt for life and the suppression of the life force itself appears to have become so self-evident that there is no cause to be surprised when this finds its ultimate expression in weapons powerful enough to destroy all human life. In short, I am in a minority, and I always have been—in the family, with my parents, with Karl. And I am repeatedly in danger of destroying the vitality in me to alleviate my loneliness. But this is over now. Earlier, I was prepared to pay any price for family harmony, to celebrate Christmas the way everyone did, packing lovely little parcels, decorating the house, dreaming up wonderful recipes. I reveled in the shining eyes of my children as they unpacked their presents, I believed I was a better mother than mine had been, I fooled myself with consummate success. I took the vow of silence, suffered without knowing why, and gradually lost contact with myself. Then came my serious illness, the liberating tears in hospital, my therapy, and the realization that lies cannot save me. Now I have no choice. I cannot hide the truth from myself, I cannot keep it away from those around me, much as I would like to because of my loneliness. But your visit today, Nina, has confirmed me in my conviction that self-denial would not extricate me from this loneliness but probably make it even worse—though in a different way. If, in the presence of others, I force myself not to see or tell the truth, then the feeling of loneliness only becomes more acute. I have my diary, and I have rare moments like the evening I spent with you today, Nina, times when I learn that there is such a thing as genuine contact that does not phase out the truth and makes me happy for that reason. As I say this, I realize that last year I had occasional encounters of this kind, not only with my children but also with other people who are lonely for the same reason, who attempt to live with the fact and for that reason can do without pretense. Why is this not enough?

3

We did not celebrate Christmas together. You preferred to spend the vacation with friends. I felt very lonely, but I was glad that you decided as you did.

But today we met, and it brought home to me how painful it used to be for me to find myself in artificial and inauthentic situations. This feeling reminds me of the early years of my life, which I spent alone with my mother, constantly forced to display feelings I never had because that was what she needed so badly. And with the unerring instinct of an orphan forced to find a substitute wherever she could find it, she actually managed in a short space of time to make me into an attentive, sensitive child employing all that child's responsiveness and learning capacity to indelibly imprint her mother's features on her mind, to register the slightest changes, notice the tiniest hints of dissatisfaction, and attempt to avoid them in future. In all those years in the orphanage my mother probably never found one single person of the kind she made me into. I not only responded with seismographic sensitivity to all her emotional ups and downs, I also did my best to spare her any unpleasantness. More than anything, I was always there when she needed me. If she didn't need me, I was all alone. Then she would leave me in the care of people who scared me and disappear for hours to give educational instruction to the staff of various orphanages. She presumably knew exactly what children in such homes really need. After all, she had been through it all herself. But she probably lacked the imagination to realize that I, her firstborn daughter, might also be in need. She was always back punctually to breast-feed me, which she did for nine months. This was her vision of Paradise. Her own mother died at her birth, and in the first few months in hospital she was bottle-fed by various nurses. What she did now was to make me into an orphan as well, a rather special kind of orphan, left to the ministrations of many different people I neither knew nor trusted. For her breast-feeding she expected that poor little orphan to be grateful all her life. Breast-feeding was not merely a gift bestowed on me. My mother would never have dreamed of wasting time on just being with me without doing something useful. Time was there to be made use of in the best possible way, for my benefit of course. It was there for the purposes of upbringing, later for my ongoing education. I was to get the best of everything. Much later, after you were born, my mother told me that she would read her educational literature while she was breast-feeding me so that my upbringing would be as perfect as possible. If she wasn't reading, she used the time to observe my behavior and teach me good manners: not to drink too quickly, not to be too greedy, not to flail around impatiently with my hands, and above all to make sure she stayed in a good mood. She proudly told me later what a perfectly behaved child she had been. In the orphanage she soon learned to perform the tasks allotted to her in double-quick time, and she received special praise for her ability to do two things at once if necessary. I was twenty-six when my mother told me all this. I sat there with you, Nina, in my arms, and very briefly I felt monstrous anger rising in my gullet. But I suppressed it immediately. How could I have told this orphan who was so proud of her achievements: "You did me real harm with your conscientious breast-feeding, and I hate you for it." I couldn't hate her. I felt sorry for her; I didn't want to hurt her. I thought that perhaps it was not only her "good upbringing" but also her own personal experience that she was passing on to me. In the first three months of her life she was fed in hospital by a number of different nurses, who undoubtedly had all kinds of other things to do as well. How was she to know that a child needs its breast-feeding mother as a refuge, as a protection against the outside world, that it learns to trust the world through her smile, her attention, her tranquility? How was my mother to know the significance of such reassurance if she had never received it herself? I was sorry for her, but the silence imposed on me rankled all the same. So I tried a compromise. I decided to broach the matter from a theoretical perspective. I tried to explain to my mother what breast-feeding means for a child, but my explanations fell on deaf ears. My mother's insensitive response hurt me so much that the words stuck in my throat. I swore never to try to explain anything to her again. Today I am the mother of grown-up children, I know this kind of silence from the other side, and the missed opportunities for an exchange still hurt. There was no point in going on talking to my mother because I was always alone when I did so. I ought to have addressed her when I was distressed, but I didn't feel that distress clearly enough. I couldn't have told her what she had done to me because at that time I didn't know. Everything that followed had to be suffered in silence.

4

When we meet and you tell me what I was to you when you were small, I see more and more clearly the misery of my own child-hood. A few years ago I attempted to be open with my mother and to explain why I had visited her less often in the period after her divorce from your father. I said: "You know, Mommy, I sometimes think that I've only started living these last few years. Before that it was as if I were dead. Can you imagine that? When I come to see you, I feel like that all over again, because I cannot be the way I now am. I don't have the freedom to tell you how differently I see things now because everything seems to scare you. I have to spare you, like in my childhood, and that depresses me. I really have to force myself to come and see you." Imagine, Nina, what she said in reply: "That's not true, Martha. I don't want you dead, I just want you the way you used to be." Don't laugh, Nina. This is what my reality looks like. How would you have responded? Wouldn't you have given up at that point? But I didn't want to give up so easily; I persisted. I said: "But that's just it. I am no longer the way I used to be. I just told you that looking back it feels like I was dead. And you tell me how much you long for the daughter who felt that way. What am I supposed to make of that, Mommy? Have you been listening? Do you realize how monstrous I find what you have just told me? It confirms everything I always sensed but cannot explain to you. You don't love the person I am, you love a replica. You didn't want me as I was, you wanted to stifle my vitality, and you succeeded for a long time. Now you can't force me anymore, you can't blackmail me, I don't have to come and see you if it costs me too much strength. But not doing so makes me suffer, perhaps more than you." She did not reply. She was an old woman, and I felt guilty because she was so frail. I thought she needed my help. But that just put me back in the same situation as when I was small. I didn't have to go and see her, but I couldn't get away from the fact that she was inside me, that she envied me for not being an orphan whose mother hadn't breast-fed her. There was nothing I could do to stop her holding that against me and ignoring my feelings. Today, I still carry that mother inside me because she ensconced herself there so early. In a sense, she took possession of me with the milk she gave me, and perhaps it will always be that way.

IT'S PAST MIDNIGHT, and I'm still writing to you, Nina. Initially, I just wanted to get things down on paper before you arrived so that I could understand better why I was afraid of your visit. Now I've started writing about my mother, and there's so much to be said that I have to go on. It is like winning you back, but in a different way. I no longer need to make use of you by telling you about my past; I can leave you your freedom and still communicate my thoughts to you. I shall write to you, Nina, and imagine the kind wisdom in your eyes as I do so. I'm not sure whether this will always be enough, but for the moment it is doing me good. I can tell you everything; I don't have to spare you or fear that I am abusing you. My mother was an orphan, and she made an orphan out of me. But at the same time, she made me into a caring "mother" for herself. And I have made you into my "mother," though it was the last thing I wanted. It was so wonderful to have your warmth and your understanding in my loneliness that it took me a long time to realize what I was doing. Luckily, you realized it. You not only told me; you firmly refused to join in the game any longer. That was good for me as well, because now I am confronted with my past in an entirely different way. It was something I spared myself even during my analysis, as long as I could make you into a mother who was better than my own. But in that way I nearly destroyed your life, despite the love I feel for you. I am convinced that this is true now that I sense so much more clearly how the concern for my mother's welfare eroded my own life.

5

Dear Nina, you have said you'll be coming to see me this evening, and I am writing as if my life were at stake. I have realized on more than one occasion that writing helps to alleviate my despair. I shall never give you this diary to read. That reminds me of the painter Emil Nolde, who painted "invisible pictures" during the Nazi era. I started addressing you in this diary when the fear of your accusations was getting stronger all the time.

Today things have changed. There is no outward reason for me to expect accusations from you, but I am still afraid, and I ask myself what it is that I fear. At first glance, the answer appears to be simple. Of course, I do not want to confront you with my despair. I want to put a cheerful face on things. I want to be the kind of mother you always wanted, carefree and well able to shoulder her destiny without your help. You have a right to expect this. From the outset you sensed the burden weighing down on me, sooner and more keenly than I did, and now you've had enough. I have understood all that, and I'm glad you were able to make it so clear to me. But why do I still believe that I have to be cheerful?

Why can't I be the way I am? I don't have to burden you with it, after all. I have the right to be distressed without appealing to you for help. But do I really? And above all, am I able to do it? Once again the image of my mother rears up between us.

Last night I dreamt of her. I was supposed to visit her because she was seriously ill, but I kept on avoiding her. I kept on ending up in rooms she had just left. We took a long time to find each other. Then a woman took me into a room and told me to wait there for someone. And in that room was my mother, sitting on a chair. Now the confrontation with her was unavoidable. I looked at her and did my best to be honest. I said: "I wanted to visit you, but then again I didn't want to. I was avoiding you, I didn't want to see you." As I said that, my mother's features darkened, her face went red and blotchy, her eyes expressionless. I felt a terrible sense of guilt, I felt like a murderess, as if I had actually killed her by telling her about my feelings. Then I heard myself say: "No, Mommy, of course I wanted to see you, I really was on my way." Immediately, her face was transformed, she looked cheerful, vital, young, and I was reassured. I also felt something like love for her and gratitude. The gratitude was for having a mother again, for not being left alone by her death, for being able to save her life. I woke up in the middle of the night. It was four o'clock, and I was dead tired, but I couldn't get back to sleep. I had brought my mother back to life, but at what price? Once again I had denied myself, pretending to be a different kind of daughter so that she was not mortally offended and could regain her equilibrium. I had managed to save my mother, but at the expense of my own truth.

It would be so much easier to live with all this, Nina, if I could carry on doing the same with you, if you hadn't refused point-blank. That way I could have ignored what had really happened to me. But you are thirty years old, and you say: "I don't want to carry your burdens anymore, I have enough of my own." And you're right. But I remain alone with my mendacious morality, and there is no one I can turn to for support. I had to conceal my suffering from my mother—my pain, my anger, my despair—so that she would not leave me, so that she would not die or withdraw into her resentment. That was why I was forced to stay silent when I most needed my mother, in the time before I could speak. My whole body wanted to cry for help, to shake her up, to appeal to her, to draw her attention to my loneliness. But because she found that so threatening, it would have been mortally dangerous for me. So at a very early stage I had to suppress the signals emitted by my body and condemn it to silence if I didn't want to die.

NOW I UNDERSTAND why I am agonizing over the question of whether I will be able to hide my despair from you when you come, Nina. Obviously I am still making you into my mother, a mother who would be completely annihilated if she were confronted with her daughter's feelings. In your presence I still feel like a little baby who would be punished with death if it did that. I keep on having to tell myself, quite consciously, that I am now an adult, that I have a right to my despair, that the appeals I once suppressed are now clamoring so loudly for attention because they were prohibited when I was a child. In this I am more or less successful. But what I rarely manage to do is to separate you from the image of my mother that I carry around inside me. All the reawakened needs I had to suppress so early are directed first of all at you, of all people. I must get it clear in my mind that any person other than you would be a more suitable candidate for the fulfillment of those needs because you are my child and not my mother.

The doorbell rings, my heart is beating, and I hope that you will not suspect how much I have been crying today.

6

Dear Nina, we've talked for hours, and I can hardly believe how you've changed. You were so relaxed, you told me so much about the life you're living, and I sensed that you were not making any special effort, you were spontaneous and genuine. This is all the more miraculous because in line with my childhood patterns our meeting today should by all the laws have been a terrible disaster. Before you arrived I was in despair and felt the mute cries for help from my time as a baby more strongly than ever before. All my fears warned me that you would find this particularly objectionable. You had told me yourself that you no longer wanted to help me solve my problems. So why, today of all days, did I feel that I was not preying on your nerves at all? You even said that I seemed much more at ease than I had been for a long time. And I was not playing a role. The only explanation I can find is that this morning I had such an acute sense of the way I had clung to my mother as a child and feared worrying and offending her that it was no longer necessary to burden you with it. Gradually, I am convinced that I only put a strain on you and ask too much of you when I expect you to hear my mute infant cries that I do not want to hear myself. Today, I did hear them, so I was able to relieve you of the task.

ENCOURAGED BY THIS experience, I have decided to go on writing. I see now that this diary is helping me to discover and come to terms with many things, as long as I am guided in my writing by my strongest feelings. For a long time I refused to realize that these feelings are bound up with you, because I prohibited myself from gratifying my childish needs by projecting them onto you. Yet this expectation reasserted itself continuously. Now I believe I have found the solution, at least for the moment. As long as I do not show you this diary, I can allow myself any feeling, and I now see clearly that those feelings ultimately lead back to my parents. I am glad that I have found this solution. When I think of my parents, I have no desire to accuse, no claims, no wishes, or if I do, it is a purely intellectual thing. Everything that has remained childlike in me falls silent when I imagine my parents, probably in much the same way that I was forced to be silent as a child so as to spare them my claims for attention. But when I think of you, Nina, those expectations surface automatically. My immediate urge is to phone you and tell you how awful I feel, how much I need you, to ask for your advice and help. This is something that I never allow myself to do, but little good has come of it. This ban only cemented the silence I imposed on myself with my parents as the only way of surviving. There was no way out, no progress, no change. I wanted to be a good mother and not put a strain on you. But in fact I was being a good *daughter* determined not to ask too much of her parents. In this diary I am finding my voice, first with you because with you I am capable of feeling. But gradually a dialogue is beginning to establish itself with my mother. It is as if I were confronting her with the way I really was. Sometimes this detour is successful, sometimes a complete failure. But I intend to go on trying because I have learned something absolutely crucial from this experience: I only pass my destiny on to you when I refuse to bear it myself. This is easily said. But how difficult it is in your mid-fifties to bring back to life the child you once were! How I would have preferred to foist this off onto you, with the argument that you are stronger than I am, less alone, and that you have all your life before you! But when I remind myself that such arguments merely serve to cover up a wrong, that I would ultimately be presenting you with a check for you to pay on behalf of your grandmother, then I fear that at fifty you might end up in the situation I am in now. And I don't want that to happen. I don't want you footing this bill. Reality must not be camouflaged, otherwise it will repeat itself.

7

Dear Nina, I ask myself why the truth is so hard to bear. Why do we always want to deceive ourselves and others? Many things in my life are only comprehensible when I look back to my childhood. Accordingly, I try to put myself in the position of a little child forced to repress the truth about its parents and its own feelings in order to survive. This has helped me realize that later in life such a person can never believe that he or she is worthy of being loved the way they are, with all their feelings and needs. They feel obliged to hide their genuine face and instead display characteristics that are quite the opposite of the way they truly feel: generosity, self-sacrifice, unselfishness. But how disappointed they are when others take them at face value! They feel exploited and ignored because no one has divined and fulfilled their secret wishes. The plan misfires. They expect to be loved for this charade, but one day they realize that no love has been forthcoming. Instead, they stand dumbfounded in the face of reality, the claims and interests of others that they refused to recognize as such. They feel cheated and badly treated.

My own past has made me very allergic to attitudes like these.

They make me intolerant because at much too early a stage I sensed the expectations lurking behind my mother's protestations of love. As I felt obliged to gratify those expectations without being able to do so, I now find myself relapsing into that early distress when I encounter such attitudes. Other people's pretense makes me afraid. Like a small child, I depend on them to be sincere. Then some people believe I am making moral claims. But that only makes me even lonelier because I feel misunderstood. I have no desire to appeal to morality because I have suffered too much from it. So what do I expect from others? When I try to give an honest answer to this question, I suddenly feel afraid. It is the fear of having to tell my mother that I see through her insincerity, that I do not believe in the façade she has erected for herself, that as a child I sensed the hatred, the anger, and the envy she was trying to conceal from me. I feel the fear of having to say to her: "You are not as good as you pretend to be. You do not love me. You are incapable of love. I despair of your insincerity and stupidity. You think you know me but all you know is my façade, my well-adjusted, smiling infant face that you believe to be my true face. But that infant face is your work. It is like the "mirror, mirror on the wall" in the fairy tale. You expect it to tell you that you are the best and wisest mother in the whole world. But behind that mirror is my true self, the perceptive eyes within me that can see the extent of my infant despair. If the characters in the fairy tale can survive a hundred years asleep, why should I not survive my fifty years in prison? I am just waking up. I am beginning to talk to you; it is not too late. You cannot put up any new walls around me, I will not let you. And the old walls are beginning to crumble."

Now, for the first time, I have been able to say straight out, without mincing my words, what I always wanted to say to my mother.

I am surprised how painful it was. How often have I thought that other women were putting up a pretense, hiding something from me that I had no right to perceive or put a name to, because it was their business and they were entitled to act that way. But on each and every such occasion I always experienced the pain it caused me to fight my perceptions, hold my tongue, and protect others from what I had clearly seen. That pain was easier to withstand than the pain I feel now. My whole body cringes at the thought that I saw through my mother with my infant eyes, perhaps even when she was changing my diapers and put her hand over my mouth, my throat, or my chest to stop me crying because she couldn't stand for me to do that. She even told me that later quite frankly, because she thought nothing of it. At the time, I had no feeling, but now I feel the grip of her hand on my throat, and I want to cry out: "Mommy, let me go! I'm afraid you'll kill me. Let me at least cry out so that someone can come to my aid, our aid. Your eyes frighten me, you look quite crazy, dealing with a baby is too much for you. Leave it to others, don't torment me. Can't you see that I'm suffering, can't you sympathize with me even a little bit? Where are your eyes, your common sense, your ears? Can't you hear the distress in my wailing? Can you perhaps not understand distress at all because you were not allowed to cry in the orphanage? How can I show you my distress except by crying? But you forbid me to do just that. Everything must stay as it was. You think it was right and proper the way you were treated as a child, and now you're training me to think the same. I feel as if I'm at the mercy of this insane idea, but no one comes to my rescue. I'm not allowed to cry for help. I can only try to tell you my distress with the expression in my eyes, but you won't look me in the face, you look away. You're preoccupied with my upbringing."

What a good thing it is, Nina, that I shall never show you this diary, that no one will ever have to read what it says. Otherwise, I might never have found out so much about myself and others. To be able to speak to my mother as a little child, I first had to break down all my inner contacts, including those with you. But I think it's been worth it. My mother stands before me more clearly every day, in all her misery, but also in all the devastation she spread around her, definitely without wanting to, in the sincere aware-ness of her duty, convinced that this was the right way to bring up a child because it was what she had learned. How often I felt that my life was in danger, how often I felt condemned to silence, condemned not to be allowed to see! How often have I tried—not without success—to free myself from these prisons. And now I stumble upon the first of those prisons, my mother's hands on my little body, preventing me from crying. Why did no one come to my aid? What was going on in my father's mind? Did he not see that I needed help?

HOW COULD HE? In the first few years of his life, all that his severely disturbed mother could communicate to him was her own fear. If I had not had to learn so early to hold my tongue what-ever happened, I might have found a way of expressing what this child always wanted to say to her father, the things that turned up repeatedly in my adult dreams without my ever taking them seriously: "Daddy, don't run away from me, don't confuse me with your sick, demanding mother. The fear in my eyes is not the same as you felt in your childhood. I'm your daughter, I'm at the mercy of my mother's insane ideas, just as you were when you were small. Don't leave me on my own, let me feel that you can see what's going on, give me the hope that I'm not entirely alone, let me tell you how

I feel! Listen to me, don't run away! I'm not putting any pressure on you, I just want to ask you some questions, and I need you to give me an answer. I need your explanations. I don't understand Mommy, and I don't understand your behavior. I don't know why you evade me, why you look away, why you don't protect me from her. You're a big, strong man; I'm just a little child. How can you leave me with her, how can you find it in your heart not to help me, not to save me? If you can't help me, then at least tell me why. I can't stand this uncertainty. I can't believe that you hate me although you caressed me so tenderly yesterday. What have I done to make you care so little for me? Is it that the love and tenderness you've given me wasn't meant for me at all? Are you not interested in my soul, my inner being, but only in my body that gives you secret feelings of pleasure? But I'm not a doll or a puppet, I'm a human being, a person, even though I'm so small. I have my own feelings, wishes, needs, and I have fears that I cannot help but show you. Look and see! I'm in mortal danger, I need help, now, not tomorrow or later, not from other people, but from you. Where are you? You stand there not saying a word. How am I to understand why you won't help me? I cannot believe that you don't care. I'd rather believe that you want to destroy me, like Mommy, because I've hurt you in some way. Then I could try to find out what it was, I could recognize my guilt and make up for it. If I did everything right, I could hope that I still might earn your love. Won't you tell me how I need to behave to get you to look at me and talk to me? I'll do whatever you want, my little body is ready for anything. I want to help you so that you'll finally be able to help me. But all my efforts are futile as long as you don't say anything. My whole body is incredibly tense. It all seems so pointless and at the same time so unspeakably tiring. It's too much for me, but I cannot give up the hope that you will help me. Take me in your arms, look in my eyes, say that you see the fear in them, that you can face up to it, that you are no longer the confused little child of a severely disturbed mother but my father, who will reassure and protect me. I must be able to rely on your help. But I do not have that certainty, my body knows so much more than I can face up to. It knows that you often touch me in the night, that I am a plaything for you. You frighten me because you do forbidden things with me. I cannot understand it. I'm glad when you touch me because Mommy only touches me to change my diapers and smear me with pungent-smelling ointment. Your hands are not rough, they are tender, and I'm so starved of tenderness. But your touch still hurts me, I feel the pain of it all through my innermost being. I'd like to yell out for the pain of it, but I mustn't. Mommy has successfully taught me that I must be silent."

You see, Nina, that pain remained stuck in my throat; for fifty years it possessed itself of my body and spread out to infect every part of it. My whole body hurt, my back, my stomach, my arms and legs. I hoped for understanding from my doctors as I had hoped for it from my father. But how could I have explained something to those strangers that I couldn't explain to my father? All those years I didn't know what the real pain was. It is the pain of being degraded as a person, of seeing my love betrayed and my trust exploited, the pain caused by my father's abuse of his power and his abuse of my body to satisfy his lusts. It is the horror at his ruthlessness and his indifference to my fear and the future course of my life, which he destroyed by interfering with my body without thinking twice about it. Am I to regard his infinite ignorance as an excuse for everything that happened back then? As a little child, I could have shown him my feelings if he had had eyes to see and ears to hear. I would have liked to tell him that his caresses seared my soul in the same way as my mother's ointments seared my skin. How I wanted him to look at me when he caressed me, to talk to me, to tell me I needn't be afraid, to explain to me what I didn't understand, to see in my eyes the pain he was inflicting on me! How I longed for a father who was not interested in my genitals but in my face, who would stroke my head, give me courage, assure me of his help, who instead of fiddling with me in silence would be in harmony with his eyes and words! I so passionately longed for my father's gaze, for him to talk to me, to establish spiritual and emotional contact with me. I do not know who my father was.

8

Today, Nina, I have the impression that I have been doomed for the rest of my life to try to find out who my father was. When I was sixteen, I did nothing to stop one of my teachers at school from abusing me sexually. I denied this violation to myself, persuaded myself that I loved him, never confessed to myself that I had sought protection from him in the hope that he would not ask for anything in return. I never noticed how high the price was that I paid at the time. I did my best not to feel the protest, the disappointment, the anger, and the pain caused by the silence imposed on me. I wanted to get over all that very quickly so as to be a worthy partner for him. Had I not made the same attempt with my father? In vain. With all these efforts I was denying my own self, forsaking my feelings, running roughshod over myself. It was a price I paid more than once. I had to foot the same bill over and over again. And every time my anger welled up, but I was unable to identify its true origins. Only now I am getting nearer those origins. They lie with you, Daddy. You took the secret with you to the grave. You denied me the explanation I now have to find all on my own. Why was I always at pains to do what people expected of me and never disappoint them? Because I hoped it would release me from the loneliness that I always experienced as a mortal danger. But I remained lonely and disappointed. I suffered from tormenting feelings of guilt that made me feel responsible for everything. The voice of those guilt feelings asked me again and again: "Why did you trust that teacher? You should have recognized all the signals telling you that he wouldn't help you. How could you believe him and throw away your body on someone who didn't love you and never even saw the person you really are?" I tried to defend myself. I had believed and hoped that he loved me. He told me so often enough, and I needed that faith in his love. But the voice of guilt knows no mercy. It speaks in the tone of my mother, for whom nothing that I did was ever good enough because I was unable to free her of her misery. So the voice drones on inexorably: "When you were sixteen, you wrote intelligent essays. How could you be so stupid as to believe that this married teacher with two children would ever leave his family for your sake? Where was your common sense? You were always so critical, not least of yourself, you read all those books, and you still fell foul of a seducer like some clueless, unenlightened girl in the nineteenth century." And that voice was right. I should have seen that he had other girls, that at my age I could never be a genuine partner for him. At school he only helped me as long as he needed me, and he soon lost interest in me after I had slept with him. All he wanted was another proof of his prowess as a seducer.

I sense now that I am imperceptibly siding with my mother's

voice, accusing myself and feeling once again as if I were in court. But I also hear a still, small voice trying to defend me: "It wasn't your fault; he alone is responsible for what happened. How could you have seen through his lies and perversions, if such lies and perversions were all you knew? How could you have known what love really is, that you have a right to respect, to ask questions and be heard? That you are not forced to be silent? That you have a right to rebel, to protest, to look things in the face, to unmask lies, and to keep your secrets to yourself? You didn't know you had any rights because your parents never let you have them. They didn't give you the key with which you could have opened your prison cell; they even hid it from you."

And that is precisely how it was. From the outset I had to learn from my mother not to use my feelings as signals, to suppress my needs and fears. I had to learn that I was not allowed to help myself. That was why I was completely dependent on help from my father, who could have saved me and given me back my integrity and made up for those mutilations. Just because I survived, I always thought of him as my savior. Maybe he did save my life, but not for my sake, only because he was interested in that little girl's body. He needed me defenseless. I was sent out into the world without rights, unarmed, with only my fear as a companion. I defended myself as best I could, but the pattern was always the same: I sought help from men who exploited me, and then I blamed myself for my naïveté and blindness. Basically, that's how it was with my marriage too. But how could I have seen what was really going on? I had been programmed to be blind at such an early stage, and I never had any chance to make comparisons. I would never have fallen for that teacher if my father had supported, respected, and seen me for what I am instead of treating me like a doll. I would immediately have seen the difference between my father's behavior and the behavior of the teacher, who would probably never have tried to approach me.

9

That still, small voice inside me is gradually developing into the strong, firm, convincing voice of an adult, and it gives me strength. I see so much more now. How it made me suffer that I could never ask Hans, my teacher, any questions, just as I could never ask my father anything or later my husband. I wanted to know what Hans felt about his marriage, the relationship he had with his children. But such questions were taboo, and I accepted that. I wanted nothing more dearly than a genuine exchange, but in the end I agreed to a mute sexual relationship. Once again I see that I am in danger of accusing myself and asking: How could you put up with it? But that voice inside is starting to defend me from self-blame. I had no choice. Right at the beginning of our affair Hans told me one or two things about himself, the disappointments in his life, and his difficult childhood. He even broke down in tears. I hoped that I could help him, that I could free him from his misery by offering him understanding and attention. After what I had been through, I was unable to gauge how much of this was calculated, part of a plan to seduce me. At sixteen I was starved of love and affection, and there was nothing I wanted more than to give someone my love in the way that only I could. I wanted to offer Hans all the gifts of my heart and my understanding because I sensed that he too was suffering. But it was beyond my power to see him as he really was. He could neither understand himself nor me, all he could do was get girls into bed and then cast them aside, whatever the reasons for his behavior may have been. But I was accustomed not to feel my distress, I wanted to help him, and I hoped he would save me. As with my father, I probably wanted to make him into someone who was able to save me. I see now that this never works. But I must stop blaming myself; otherwise I shall end up being loyal and faithful both to him and to my father. And that loyalty will keep me locked up in the old prison cell that no one can free me from because I have taken the guilt of others on myself. Like Joan of Arc, who squandered herself on an imbecile king, I will end up killing myself rather than betraying my father. Is that what I want? No. I shall not let myself be destroyed by feelings of guilt. I shall not be the keeper of other people's secrets. I refuse to save the culprits by destroying myself.

THE BIGGEST CULPRIT is my father. It was from him I learned never to ask questions, to live with his evasions, never to cause him trouble, never to reveal his insecurity. I had to believe in his good intentions, turn a blind eye to the rottenness and vindictiveness in him, smile at him, and let him play his perverted games with my body. For none of this was he accountable to me; in fact, I was accountable to him. At my expense he could swagger and strut. He behaved like a king, giving me commands and imposing his will on me. I had to condone his jealousies, overlook his lies, tolerate his weakness and cowardliness, commiserate with his illness, cover up his alcoholism. One word from me about his drinking habits would have put him in a towering rage. And where would that have left me with my puny little illusions about having a father who loved me? I needed those illusions in order to survive, like the air I needed to breathe. I had a mother who had no love or warmth to give me, who panicked in the face of my feelings and needs. Those are the facts. I could not do without my father, so I had to avoid arousing his anger, I had to submit to my fate, I had to be silent, affectionate, well-behaved, and easy to handle, I had to be blind and stupid—all this so as not to undermine the shaky foundations of his character. And I succeeded. I actually managed to graduate with flying colors from university and still remain stupid. And though I became quite a militant feminist for a time, deep down I was still the anxious little girl trembling before her drunken father's fits of temper but still longing for the father I never had when I was small, still unable to do without the image of a loving father because she could neither see through nor perceive the abuse inflicted on her in the first years of her life. But now I have a clear picture of what really happened. It hurts more than I ever thought it could. But this realization still gives me strength. Seeing my parents more clearly and facing up to them has made me ready to leave my subterranean prison and give up my blindness. I no longer believe that blindness and silence can save my life, because an existence like that does not deserve the name of life. How many people, men and women, stay silent because they were exposed so early to the threat of being killed if they opened their mouths? But a life like that is a martyrdom that most of us probably never even sense because we have not been allowed to see it for what it is.

I REALIZE NOW, Nina, that I am no longer addressing my words to you. I no longer need to tell you about my sorrow and my distress. I am getting closer to my past, and I am learning to withstand the feelings that come welling up in the process. Of course, it would be marvelous if you could understand me. But the main thing is that I understand myself, which means that I am no longer so dependent on your understanding. That is why I no longer need to burden you with my pain. I don't need you to save me. Perhaps one day you might like to hear my story, which after all is part of your story. Maybe then we can talk about it freely without putting any pressure on you. You are living your own life much more strongly now that you have freed yourself of the role you had to play for me for so long. I am glad. It has given me the opportunity to face up to myself and my own story.

Notes

1
Depression: Compulsive Self-Deception

1 Elsbeth Wolffhcim, *Anton Tschechow*, trans. A. J. (Hamburg: Rowohlt, 2001), p. 13.
2 Ibid., p. 14.
3 Ibid., p. 15.
4 See Alice Miller, *The Body Never Lies* (New York: W. W. Norton, 2005), pp. 45–46.
5 Ivan Bunin, *Tschechow* (Berlin: Friedenauer Presse, 2004).
6 See Alice Miller, *Thou Shalt Not Be Aware* (New York: Farrar Straus, and Giroux, 1984).
7 *Nicolas de Staël* (Paris: Éditions du Centre Pompidou, 2003).

3
How Does Evil Come into the World?

1 Michel Odent, *The Scientification of Love* (London: Free Association, 1999).

6
Private Mania

1 Alice Miller, *For Your Own Good* (New York: Farrar, Straus and Giroux, 1983).
2 See Alice Miller, *Breaking Down the Wall of Silence* (New York: Meridian, 1993).
3 Daniel Goldhagen, *Hitler's Willing Executioners* (New York: Knopf, 1996).
4 See Alice Miller, *Breaking Down the Wall of Silence* (New York: Basic Books, 2009).

11
Taking It Personally: Indignation as a Vehicle of Therapy

1 See James Gilligan, *Violence: Our Deadly Epidemic and Its Causes* (New York: Putnam, 1996).
2 Frank M. Lachmann, *Transforming Aggression* (Northvale, NJ: J. Aronson, 2000).

References

"The Wellsprings of Horror" was first published as "Woher kommt das Grauen?" in the *Frankfurter Allgemeine Zeitung*, 6 October 2001.

"Private Mania" is based on a lengthy discussion with Thomas Gruner on "children and society" in 2004. The original version can be found on my Web site under "Interviews."

"Ideal Soldiers: When Will We No Longer Need Them?" was first published as "Wann gibt es endlich keine idealen Soldaten mehr?" in *Weltwoche*, 21 February 1991.

"The Tragedy of Jessica": This article was offered to *Spiegel* magazine, but the editors refrained from publishing it "because we have already covered the case so exhaustively." This is another instance of forgoing the opportunity for drawing conclusions from cases like this and enlightening readers on the reasons for such allegedly inexplicable murders.

"The Feeling Child" is a revised and abridged version of an interview with therapist Diane Connors published in *Omni* magazine under the title "The Roots of Violence" and also to be found on the Web site www.naturalchild.org/alice_Miller/roots_violence.html.

"Beyond Philosophy" is a thoroughly revised version of an interview given to a journalist who has since died. The interview has only been published on the Alice Miller Web site.

"Violence Kills Love: Spanking, the Fourth Commandment, and the Suppression of Authentic Feelings": Alice Miller talking to Borut Petrovic Jesenovec for the Slovenian magazine *ONA*, June 2005.

"Combating Denial" is an interview with Borut Petrovic Jesenovec, July 2005.